Comments on other *Amazing Stories* from readers & reviewers

"You might call them the non-fiction response to Harlequin romances: easy to consume and potentially addictive."
Robert Martin, *The Chronicle Herald*

"Tightly written volumes filled with lots of wit and humour about famous and infamous Canadians."
Eric Shackleton, *The Globe and Mail*

"This is popular history as it should be ... For this price, buy two and give one to a friend."
Terry Cook, a reader from Ottawa, on **Rebel Women**

"Stories are rich in description, and bristle with a clever, stylish realness."
Mark Weber, *Central Alberta Advisor*, on **Ghost Town Stories II**

"The resulting book is one readers will want to share with all the women in their lives."
Lynn Martel, *Rocky Mountain Outlook*, on **Women Explorers**

"[The books are] long on plot and character and short on the sort of technical analysis that can be dreary for all but the most committed academic."
Robert Martin, *The Chronicle Herald*

"A compelling read. Bertin ... has selected only the most intriguing tales, which she narrates with a wealth of detail."
Joyce Glasner, *New Brunswick Reader*, on **Strange Events**

"The heightened sense of drama and intrigue, combined with a good dose of human interest is what sets Amazing Stories *apart."*
Pamela Klaffke, *Calgary Herald*

UNSUNG HEROES OF THE CANADIAN ARMY

UNSUNG HEROES OF THE CANADIAN ARMY

Incredible Tales of Courage and
Daring During World War II

MILITARY

by Cynthia J. Faryon

PUBLISHED BY ALTITUDE PUBLISHING CANADA LTD.
1500 Railway Avenue, Canmore, Alberta T1W 1P6
www.altitudepublishing.com
www.amazingstories.ca
1-800-957-6888

Extreme care has been taken to ensure that all information presented in
this book is accurate and up to date. Neither the author nor the
publisher can be held responsible for any errors.

Publisher	Stephen Hutchings
Associate Publisher	Kara Turner
Series Editor	Diana Marshall
Editors	Jill Foran and Frances Purslow
Cover and Layout	Bryan Pezzi

We acknowledge the financial support of the Government
of Canada through the Book Publishing Industry Development
Program (BPIDP) for our publishing activities.

Altitude GreenTree Program
Altitude Publishing will plant twice as many trees as were used
in the manufacturing of this product.

National Library of Canada Cataloguing in Publication Data

Faryon, Cynthia J., 1956-
   Unsung heroes of the army / Cynthia J. Faryon.

(Amazing stories)
Includes bibliographical references.
ISBN 1-55439-009-5

   1. Soldiers--Canada--Biography. 2. Canada. Canadian Army--Biography.
3. Heroes--Canada--Biography. 4. Canada. Canadian Army--History--World
War, 1939-1945. I. Title. II. Series: Amazing stories (Canmore, Alta.)

D768.15.F37 2006   940.53'71'0922   C2006-900804-3

Printed and bound in Canada by Friesens
2 4 6 8 9 7 5 3 1

To all who fought for our freedom.

To those of us who have walked the silent cemeteries and have seen the crosses marking the true cost of victory, the price seems steep indeed. All the Canadians who fought in World War II were volunteers. Those who lived, as well as those who died, gave up more than the rest of us will ever truly appreciate.
"For Matchless Gallantry"

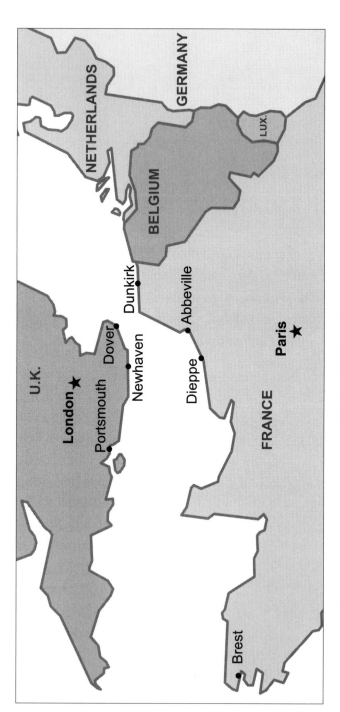

The English Channel

Contents

Prologue

All of the veterans I interviewed for this book were memorable. However, my interview with Fred Snell of Winnipeg, Manitoba, stood out among the rest. He told me about the snipers he killed after they'd wiped out half his platoon. He explained how his platoon leader had bled to death on his lap, and how he'd watched helplessly as men burned to death in their tank after hitting a land mine. With dry eyes he reiterated the stories of his war experiences, while I listened with wonder at how he could appear so unaffected — so normal. He displayed little emotion as he relived the events of 60 years ago.

Only one story managed to bring tears to his eyes, and to mine. One day his young daughter was crying as she arrived home from school. In honour of Remembrance Day, her teacher had told the class about the Canadians who fought in World War II and asked if anyone knew a hero living in their town. The students shook their heads. The teacher continued, "There is a man, the father of someone right here in this room, who won the second highest military award for bravery." Then she explained what had earned him such a distinguished award.

The little girl sobbed as she turned her tear-strewn face to her father and asked, "Daddy, why didn't you ever tell me?"

Chapter 1
So That Others May Live

I t is October 27, 1941, and the men of "C" Force are boarding the ships that will take them to the British colony of Hong Kong. A month earlier, the British had requested that Canada send troops there to deter the Japanese from attacking the colony. The Canadian government agreed to send two battalions, and now nearly 2000 men from the Royal Rifles of Canada and the Winnipeg Grenadiers are about to begin their mission.

As the ships leave Vancouver, the troops on board laugh and joke, certain they are in for an easy assignment. Most of these men have never been to battle, and many have not yet been trained with real weapons. But it doesn't matter. None of them expect to see combat over there. At this point, few believe there will be any fighting in the Pacific.

The ships arrive in Hong Kong on November 16, and the men disembark the next day. The crews on board the HMCS *Prince Robert* and the *Awatea* tell the men they will return for them after the war, and wish them a happy vacation. Everyone laughs.

For the next three weeks, it is relatively quiet in the colony. Brigadier John Lawson, commander of the West Brigade, makes sure the troops are familiar with the terrain, and that command posts are in place with supplies and land lines. He wants to be sure his men are as ready as possible, regardless of whether or not the Japanese strike.

His preparations are not in vain. On December 8, only hours after attacking Pearl Harbor, the Japanese invade Hong Kong from land, air, and sea. Pushing their way across the colony, they begin 17 days of hellish battles. The men of the Royal Rifles and Winnipeg Grenadiers become the first Canadians to fight in World War II.

Soon, the Japanese have penetrated the Gin Drinkers Line, the first Allied defence position. The Canadian defenders, along with British and Indian soldiers, quickly withdraw and take up positions on the perimeter of Hong Kong Island.

On December 18, the enemy hits the island, and the Canadians do what they can to fight back. The air is filled with enemy planes dive bombing and strafing the troops below. Enemy bullets ricochet off rocks and cut bamboo stalks in half as the Canadians fight for every bit of ground. The terrain is difficult to traverse — steep and rocky, with narrow, winding roads that hug the mountainsides. The battle is referred to as "Little Hong Kong," but to the men in its midst, this is as big as it gets.

The fighting intensifies. On the morning of December 19, "A" Company of the Winnipeg Grenadiers is ordered to take Jardine's Lookout and then Mount Butler, which rises ominously above them. The objective seems impossible; from atop the mountain, the Japanese are mercilessly hailing bullets on the men.

Things become that much worse when, in the chaos of battle, "A" Company gets divided and the groups lose radio contact with each other. Each group consists of two platoons. Second Lieutenant Charles French is in command of one group, and he and his men push on to take Mount Butler. The men are exhausted from days of fighting. They've had little or no food, and even fresh water is a scarcity. Still they fight their way upward and manage to clear Jardine's Lookout with bayonets in a bitter hand-to-hand struggle, suffering horrific losses in the process. When the fighting lessens, only 65 men remain, but they forge ahead and attack Mount Butler nonetheless. In the first few minutes of the battle for Mount Butler, the Japanese troops let loose an onslaught of rapid machine-gun fire, hitting Lieutenant French twice. The 20-year-old lieutenant bleeds to death in a matter of minutes, leaving Sergeant-Major J. R. (Jack) Osborne of Saskatchewan in command.

Overhead, Jack hears the drone of warplanes, the whistle of enemy shells, and the whine of bullets raping the air.

Jack has only moments to make his decisions — decisions that will seal the fate of his men — his comrades and fellow Canadians.

Leaving the dead and the wounded behind with the medics, Jack urges his men forward. Crouching, rolling, firing, and hitting the dirt, they struggle to gain ground through the heavy jungle and steep hillside. Jack is keenly aware that many of the men serving under him are new to war, new to their platoon, and new to the weapons they hold in their hands. He is determined to keep them alive.

The humidity is thick; it hangs in the air, mixing with the stench of spent explosives and fresh blood from the wounded. While the jungle's foliage provides moderate cover from enemy planes, it also gives Japanese ground troops and snipers places to hide. With heightened senses, the Canadians push forward, constantly looking up, to the sides, and behind — ever conscious of the enemy around them.

Concealed in bushes and trees, the Japanese open fire and drive the Canadians back a few metres. Camouflaged and blending in with their surroundings, the enemy seems to be everywhere at once. Jack rallies his men and, firing in all directions, they push forward again, gaining little ground before unremitting bullets stop them once more.

Meanwhile, enemy planes diving from above strafe the area, cutting through the undergrowth and hitting the ground, sending dirt flying. Jack's group fights their way to the top of the mountain, but their jubilance lasts only a few moments before the Japanese resume their attack. The Canadians manage to hold the peak for more than three hours; then the situation becomes desperate. The enemy has all but wiped out the group, leaving only 30 Grenadiers able to fight.

Jack's orders are to take and hold Mount Butler, but whenever his men manage to eliminate an enemy soldier, two more take the fallen warrior's place. Realizing withdrawal is the only logical option, Jack orders a retreat to safer ground. Covering them with a continual hail of bullets, he sends his men down the hill a few at a time, to join the rest of "A" Company.

Bit by bit, the men safely reach the bottom of the hill, joining the larger group of Grenadiers gathered there. After sending off the last few men, Jack stands alone against the enemy. He provides a diversion to give his fleeing men a better chance. Crouching, firing, diving from rock to tree, he draws the enemy fire. As soon as the last man is safe, Jack spins and makes a mad dash through a hail of bullets, slipping and sliding downward, and finally joins his men at the base of the hill.

The reprieve is short-lived. The larger group is in the same situation that Jack's group had been in at the top of the hill, and it's decided they must withdraw and regroup at Wong Nei Chong. But the enemy has completely cut off the Allies, and with the ocean at their backs, the company has nowhere to go. As the enemy advances, Jack's group finds refuge in a small gully.

As Jack pokes his head up over the edge of the gully, he sees a grenade lobbed through the air toward them. Jack yells a warning to his men, and everyone but Jack ducks and covers as the grenade explodes close by, sending a storm of dirt and debris high into the air. Almost immediately, another grenade sails at them through the foliage, and everyone scrambles for cover. Jack, however, leaps into the air, catches the grenade, and tosses it back at the enemy. *Kaboom!*

Jack's men smile and slap him on the back. But soon another grenade flies in over the crest of the gully. Again, Jack catches it and throws it back, as his men fire in the direction of the incoming grenades. They try to hold the enemy at bay as the grenades keep coming and Jack returns them. Each man knows that unless they drive the enemy back, one of those grenades will go off in their midst — it's only a matter of time. The battle escalates as the handful of Canadians fight for their lives.

Suddenly, three grenades sail in from different directions, and Jack can't catch them all. He grasps two as the third lands at his feet with a sickening thud. Without hesitation, he throws the two in his hands and flings himself on top of the third explosive as his men watch in horror. There's a muffled explosion as Jack's body vibrates with the blast, twitches, and then lies still. The dust settles. The six surviving men of the two platoons stare in disbelief and horror at Jack's motionless body. He died so that they might live.

The enemy moves in and the remaining Canadians are taken prisoner.

Back home in Winnipeg, Jack Osborne's wife and family are preparing for Christmas dinner when the telegram arrives. They open the door to their home, and on the front step is a soldier holding the dreaded piece of paper. The prairie cold blows white clouds into the warm kitchen as snow drifts around the messenger's boots.

There is little comfort for their loss, but knowing Jack as they did, they are certain he died as he lived — selflessly and bravely.

* * *

During the battle for Hong Kong, 267 Canadians were killed and 493 wounded. Those who survived were taken prisoner by the Japanese and spent years as POWs in conditions that caused an additional 267 deaths. When released, the survivors were picked up and brought home by the same ship that had delivered some of the original 2000 men. The crew of the HMCS *Prince Robert* had promised to come back for them. It took a few years, and the men had suffered many hardships in the meantime, but in the end, the crew lived up to their promise.

Chapter 2
Massacre on the Beach

Once filled with vacationers and honeymooners, the French seaside resort of Dieppe is quiet this moonless night. The town, built along majestic cliffs overlooking the English Channel, is presently devoid of tourists and other civilians. Absent is the soft murmuring of lovers walking hand in hand along the beach and the delighted shrieks of children playing nearby. The only sound is that of the waves tumbling over the rocky shore.

Though the coastal town appears peaceful in the darkness, the quiet holds a sinister air. Hidden from view along the top of the cliffs are German guns aimed menacingly across the Channel toward England. At the base of the cliffs, lengths of barbed wire are strung along the rocky beach to discourage attackers. For those invaders undeterred by the flesh-ripping barbs, there are land mines buried under the loose shale. The two-metre-high sea wall that parallels the beach is also lined with barbed wire, and machine-gun posts dot its length.

The port of Dieppe and its surrounding coastal communities — like almost all of continental Europe — are under German occupation. The small vacation homes and hotels along the 1.2-kilometre arced coastline are filled with hundreds of German soldiers. And, zeroing in on the various beaches from rooftops, windows, and cliff tops are manned machine guns and mortars, ready to defend the shore at a moment's notice. This evening is the last of the year's highest tides. The enemy is on alert. If an Allied invasion is to come, it will be tonight.

In England, there is movement along the coastal streets in the late night hours. The Allies are amassing an army of over 6100 men and moving them under the cover of darkness to transport boats waiting off shore. Along the South Road of New Haven, tanks belonging to the 14th Canadian Army Tank Division are rumbling down the hill to board barges that will take them across the Channel. They are part of a convoy that is set to attack Dieppe before dawn.

As the tanks make their way down the road, the trembling earth awakens five-year-old Jim Still. Running to his bedroom window, Jim's eyes grow wide as he sees the heavy artillery rumbling slowly past his house. Without a sound, he runs down the stairs and out the back door for a closer look. His excitement builds as a tank slows down and stops outside his fenced yard.

Jim looks up to see a man climbing out of the hole in the top of the vehicle. The stranger jumps to the ground and beckons Jim over. "Hey son," he says. "Wanna go for a ride?"

Jim nods, and the man lifts him up onto the tank. Scrambling to the hole, Jim takes a look at his house before disappearing into the guts of the vehicle. He is placed in a seat, and all around him are levers and dials of all descriptions. Other men in the tank nod at him and then continue with what they're doing.

Jim feels very important, sitting in his chair. He can hear men talking outside, and then someone shouts an order. In response, one of the soldiers in the tank begins pushing pedals with his feet. The tank moves, and Jim's heart beats faster. He quickly leaves his seat, climbs the ladder, and pokes his head out to see what's happening. A man on the side of the road wearing a red cap sees Jim and starts to point and shout. The tank comes to a sudden stop, and the man in the red cap tells Jim to get out and go home. "War is no place for a kid," he says.

Afraid the man is going to chase him, Jim scales down the tank and runs for home. His heart is beating so hard it hurts. Glancing over his shoulder before entering his home, Jim wishes he'd asked the name of the man who had invited him inside the tank. He'd like to find him later and thank him. But Jim will never see that man or any of the others again. For the rest of his life, he will wonder what happened to that crew.

An hour later, the tanks are loaded onto a transport barge to take part in an operation that some will later claim was a suicide mission.

The plan of attack

Slipping ominously through the dark, cold waters of the English Channel, 237 Allied ships make their way to the French coastline on Wednesday, August 19, 1942. The convoy is transporting 6100 Allied troops, approximately 5000 of whom are men and officers of the 2nd Canadian Infantry Division. Commanded by Major General J. H. Roberts, this division includes the Royal Regiment of Canada, the Black Watch (Royal Highland Regiment), the Essex Scottish, the South Saskatchewan Regiment, the Queen's Own Cameron Highlanders of Canada, Les Fusiliers Mont Royal, the Royal Canadian Engineers, the 14th Canadian Army Tank Division (the Calgary Regiment), The Royal Hamilton Light Infantry, the Toronto Scottish Machine Gunners, the Medical Corps, and the Provost. Joining the men of this division are about 1000 British commandos, 50 U.S. Army Rangers, and 15 Free French soldiers.

The average age of the Canadian soldiers is 22. At home in Canada, they are fathers, brothers, sons, and uncles. In their regular lives, they go to schools and work in offices, farms, and factories across the country. But now, they are here to serve their country, and they are about to display a courage and an audacity that will shock and electrify the world.

The attack on Dieppe, code-named Operation Jubilee, is to unfold in two phases. During the first phase, assault troops land in areas west and east of Dieppe, launching surprise attacks on both flanks. Phase two begins a half hour later, when more troops launch a main, frontal attack on Dieppe itself. Each regiment, in each phase, has orders to attack certain targets, such as the harbour, enemy headquarters, and specific shore batteries. Some regiments are to act as forward troops, clearing the way for the next wave to pass through on their way to separate objectives. All troops are to be supported by the Allied air force and navy, who will provide diversions while the men land safely — and undetected — on the beaches. Once the enemy is subdued, the men are to regroup on the beaches for evacuation, leaving in the same landing crafts that delivered them.

At best, this mission will be the beginning of the end of World War II. At worst, it is a dress rehearsal for the next frontal invasion, providing the Allies with strategic information on the enemy's battle strengths and weaknesses.

In every mission, there are elements of the unexpected, and, bearing this in mind, the assault troops prepare themselves as best they can. As the convoy nears the

French coastline, the dark purple sky begins to lighten. It's a beautiful, peaceful predawn, with the sea breeze blowing the smell of the ocean across the decks of the ships. In their wake, the phosphorus is twinkling, echoing the stars in the sky above. In this serene setting, it's hard for the men to imagine that this new day will bring anything but good fortune for the Allies.

As daybreak approaches, the long, dark shadows of the ships show more plainly against the smooth water. There is an unspoken urgency to deploy the troops on the beaches before the sun comes up. The timing has to be perfect to protect the men. Once onshore, they will be at the mercy of the German guns.

Canadians on the western flank

Among the massive convoy approaching the French coastline is the transport ship HMS *Princess Beatrix*. On board this ship are the men of the South Saskatchewan Regiment, with Lieutenant Colonel Cecil Merritt commanding.

At the moment, Lieutenant Colonel Merritt, a young lawyer from Vancouver, British Columbia, is briefing his men on what to expect on the beaches. The men are silent, giving their leader their full attention. Underscoring Merritt's voice, they hear the dull throb of the ship's engines and the wash of the Channel waters. All portholes and hatches are closed and covered with blackout curtains. Below decks, the lights are blue, but no light shows on deck. From the bridge, the shadows of the other ships can just be discerned in the sea haze.

In muted tones, Merritt describes to his men the rugged coast of France and the area west of Dieppe where they will be landing. It is a beach near the town of Pourville. The regiment is expected to secure a beachhead along the Scie River's banks for the next wave of assault troops. Once this is accomplished, the South Saskatchewans' "A" and "D" Companies will make their way to Dieppe's western outskirts and take control of the nearby radar station. At the same time, "B" and "C" Companies will secure the town of Pourville itself, and then attempt to take the western cliffs above the town.

As Merritt reviews the plan, he explains that the Germans have set up guns at the top of the cliffs overlooking the shoreline, and that these guns are aimed on the beach and out toward the Channel. At this moment, the Allied air force is gathering planes from air bases across England. These aircraft will act as a noisy decoy, drawing the attention of the enemy guns up and away from the beaches, giving the first wave of troops a window of opportunity to take out the shoreline guns and lay open the harbour. The soldiers will also be supported by the navy ships dotting the coastline. After the invading army has disembarked, the ships will take up battle posts offshore to shell the German guns on the cliff tops.

After the briefing, the men are dismissed. Lost in their individual thoughts, they recheck their weapons and finish dressing for battle. The air is thick with tension. For some of these boys, this is to be their first battle, and the thought of killing other men is almost as daunting as the thought of other men trying to kill them. They all know surviving this battle will be difficult. Letters home are safely tucked away so that loved ones will have something personal if the boys don't make it back.

Soon, the order is sent down the line. The troops have been instructed to board their landing crafts. Silently, they file into the hallways and up the ladders to the top deck of the *Princess Beatrix*.

There are approximately 100 landing vessels being used in the Dieppe raid, and each one holds between 40 and 80 men. Open at the top, each of these metal boats has high sides, a machine gun in the bow, and a front panel that drops open when it's time for the troops to disembark. In ideal conditions, the landing crafts pull into a few feet of water and the soldiers wade ashore.

As Lieutenant Colonel Merritt boards his landing craft, he knows that in addition to the shadowy outlines of other landing crafts filled with foot soldiers, there are British commandos in motor launches and motor gunboats, tank men in tank landing-barges, and more infantry in huge transports. But knowing other boats are out there is little comfort inside the crowded confines of his own landing craft. The metal is cold, the smell of sweat mixes with the pungent odour of the sea, and the sound of anxious breathing is loud in his ears. Each soldier is in a world of his own as he waits for the front panel to drop. Soon it will be time to emerge into hell.

Meanwhile, those in command of the raid watch tensely from the bridges of the destroyers. Their thoughts are with their men and the daunting task before them. The mine-sweepers have swept the minefields and marked the way for the invading forces. Now, with their job done, they hang back to watch and wait in case they are needed for additional support. From each transport ship, the small landing crafts drift silently forward, one behind the other in two columns of about nine vessels each.

The first wave of landing crafts nose into shallow water at Pourville at 4:50 a.m. Unfortunately, they have drifted a bit, and most soldiers of the South Saskatchewan Regiment find themselves west of the Scie River instead of east of it. This means that Lieutenant Colonel Merritt and his men will have to fight their way across the river, losing precious time.

The long wait ends abruptly as the doors of the landing crafts drop. The first wave of Saskatchewans springs forward and runs up onto the shore. The clatter of gunfire can be heard in the distance as the guns of the Germans follow the Allied bombers, which have drawn enemy attention away from the shore, as planned. The only noise on the beach is the crunching of boots on damp pebbles — as loud to each man as a shell exploding.

Lieutenant Colonel Merritt and his men swarm the beach and come to the stone wall. Explosions fill the air as land mines are found by heavy boots, but the wave of men surges forward still. Wire-cutters are extracted to excise the coils of barbed wire barring the way. Then, ladders are leaned up against the wall. Soon, the men are over the barrier and spilling into the streets of Pourville. Still there is no sign that the Germans know of their approach, but the earth shivers with the roar of the great guns firing at the aircraft overhead. The lingering night shadows are streaked with flaming arcs from enemy guns — guns that will soon focus their sinister gaze on the shore, unless the Allies can get to them first.

Suddenly, shells that a few moments ago were whining over their heads change direction. Enemy snipers have spotted the invaders, and dirt and stones are spitting up around the Saskatchewans' feet from the impact of the bullets hitting the ground. A small group is ordered by Colonel Merritt to take cover in a mined blockhouse. Among them is Wallace Reyburn, a reporter with the *Montreal Standard.*

The small group continues to fight and give cover for other soldiers making it over the wall and into the street. Finally, the Camerons arrive, and the Saskatchewans give up the blockhouse to them. As the group leaves, the Germans blow the mines, and shrapnel flies in all directions. Many men are killed; some are wounded and evacuated back to the aid station on the beach.

Merritt and his group of Canadians dive for the dirt and roll for cover after making it over the wall, then regroup against the side of a nearby building. They crouch and weave their way slowly from house to house, searching for a strategic location to set up headquarters. They eventually find an empty hotel.

As soon as the wireless sets are working, Lieutenant Colonel Merritt orders a group of his men to move inland and take command of the bridge that spans the Scie River. Ignoring the machine guns rattling around them, Reyburn and the rest of the men break out of the hotel and shoot their way to the river. The bridge, which is well guarded by Germans, needs to be taken so that the Cameron Highlanders, who will soon be coming up from behind, can make it across the river on their way inland. Once through, the Camerons are to join with the Calgary Regiment's Churchill tanks to attack German head-quarters in the village of D'Arques. Then they are to circle around to regroup on the main beach.

While members of the Saskatchewans are making their way to the bridge, the tide is turning for the soldiers back on the beach. Germans are now picking off men in and out of the landing crafts. The machine-gun posts along the footpaths are springing to life, cutting down the exposed soldiers with deadly fire. From the cliffs, the enemy shore batteries add to the rain of bullets and men are massacred without firing a shot in their own defence. Very few make it to the village, where they battle from house to house, bush to hedge.

As the morning progresses, the battle becomes desperate. The group of Saskatchewans now at the bridge contemplate their best plan of attack. In front of them lie two machine-gun posts, one above the other, guarding the river crossing. These will have to be taken out of action.

The men rush toward the bridge, crouching, firing, rolling, and running forward again. As the enemy guns open up, some of the Canadians are mowed down. The remaining men find cover on either side of the bridge and try to rush it again. Attempt after attempt is made, but the bridge is not taken. Some of the men jump into the river, but are shot by snipers before they reach the other side. The remaining troops drop back to a nearby courtyard and send a message to battalion headquarters, reporting the strength of the German resistance.

Back at the hotel, Lieutenant Colonel Merritt is quiet. After a moment, he strides out into streets, now flooded with daylight and gunfire, and makes his way to the courtyard near the bridge. Here he finds his men gallantly trying again and again to cross the bridge, only to be driven back by enemy guns.

Lieutenant Colonel Merritt studies the bridge, taking note of the location of enemy gun posts. Then he looks at the stream blocked with his soldiers' bodies. At first glance, it seems hopeless, but Merritt has a plan. Setting his jaw and standing up straight, he calmly takes off his helmet and begins to walk toward the bridge, in full view of the enemy guns.

"Come on, men," he says encouragingly. "They can't hit us all. Don't bunch up. Here we go." Twirling his helmet, he strolls out onto the bridge. The enemy fires and blasts of dirt jump at Merritt's boots. He is unharmed and continues forward.

Hesitant at first, his men leave their hiding places and follow his lead. When one large group has crossed safely, the colonel walks back across the bridge to lead the next group across. The enemy gunfire increases on the next crossing, and a few men are hit, but the colonel continues walking calmly and swinging his helmet until this group has crossed as well.

Six times back and forth, with bullets whining and spitting at him, bursting shells deafening him, Colonel Merritt crosses the bridge.

Once across, the soldiers hit the ground at the base of the gun post. Inch by inch, they crawl up toward the enemy. The colonel and two sergeants reach it first. In unison, their arms jerk swiftly into the air as they launch three hand grenades through the slit of the lower gun post, next to the barrel projecting toward the river. An explosion rocks the earth around them, accompanied by screams and a belch of pungent smoke. Again grenades are launched, this time through the slit of the upper turret. And again the earth shudders with the blast. Both guns are now silenced.

As the dust settles, high and shrill above the tumult from the shore batteries, the skirl of bagpipes can be heard playing the "March of the Cameron Men." The Camerons of Winnipeg have arrived, and their way has successfully been cleared by Colonel Merritt and his South Saskatchewans.

Their job is done, and, leaving the others to continue on to the radar station and other objectives, Merritt, with a gun in each hand, leads the way back through the village to the beach at Pourville for the set rendezvous with the ships.

Reyburn is with the first group of men that makes it back to the beach. He has been onshore for only six and a half hours. When the boats finally come at 11 a.m., the tide is out. The men have to run nearly 275 metres to the boats under a constant hail of machine-gun bullets, mortars, and exploding shells.

Reyburn's boat gets stuck in the mud while an enemy plane hammers at them. Finally they push off, after minutes that seem like hours, and the view of the beach they are leaving behind is beyond nightmarish. Men — dead, dying, wounded — litter the beach. Others are up to their knees in the water, waiting and praying for the boats to make it in to take them away. Reyburn watches as men are cut down, and others fight back shot for shot.

Suddenly, he realizes his boat is filling with water. Within seconds, about 10 metres from shore, the boat sinks. Swimming hard, some of the men make it to a tank-landing craft. No sooner does Reyburn make it on board than this boat also begins to sink. People begin throwing everything off the craft that isn't nailed down, hoping they can make it to the next boat before this one goes under. Guns, boots, belts, everything heavy goes overboard, and finally, they make it to a small flak ship that transports them to one of the nearby destroyers.

Back on the beach, German guns relentlessly continue their hail of death. Their focus has shifted from the men below to the landing crafts coming to shore, and many vessels are hit. It soon becomes apparent that not all of the surviving troops will be able to get off the beach. The choice is made: the worst of the wounded will go first, covered by those who are still well enough to use a gun. Then once the wounded are off, if there are any seats left on the boats, it will be first come first served.

Reaching the sea wall from the streets of Pourville, Colonel Merritt and the South Saskatchewans begin their descent to the beach. Their landing crafts have not yet been able to get ashore, and the men hope they arrive soon, as the enemy's firepower is intensifying. From the cliff above, a large enemy gun continually blasts the beach. The offshore ships fire back. Some landing crafts are shelled in the crossfire and drift uselessly on the tide.

The Saskatchewans cling to the slight shelter of the sea wall while they wait for the boats. At last their rescue boats arrive, and Lieutenant Colonel Merritt orders his men to evacuate the beach in groups.

Suddenly, a thud and a whistle are heard, and the shell from a gun-post on the cliff above explodes in the midst of Merritt's group. Shell fragments and pebbles fly in all directions and the soldiers hit the sand, their screams accompanied by the continual booming of the enemy's guns. Pinned against the cliffs, the Saskatchewans are cut off from their waiting boats.

Merritt gets up from the sand, unharmed except for a gash on his face. Wiping the blood away, he looks at the carnage around him and knows that what's left of his men are looking to him for help. Peering at the cliff above, he yells for volunteers to come with him to take out that gun.

Two men grab their weapons, and the trio runs to the cliff base as flying bullets spray gravel around their feet. After scaling the wall, the three meet at the base of the shore battery. In perfect unison, they launch three grenades through the slit in the pillbox. The Canadians dive to the ground as it shudders with the force of the explosions.

Lieutenant Colonel Merritt and his men, carrying as many wounded as possible, scramble for the ships and escape the beach.

Canadians on the eastern flank

While the assault troops landing at Pourville are able to attack with the element of surprise, those landing on the eastern flank are not as lucky. Things begin going wrong for the Royal Regiment and three companies of the Black Watch long before they reach shore. A German boat spots the landing crafts as they make their approach, and immediately opens fire on the soldiers. The invaders return fire with the machine guns in the bows of their crafts, and more German boats enter the fight. An invading destroyer comes quickly to the Canadians' rescue, and the enemy retreats to sound the alarm along the coast.

Off course by a kilometre, the Royals swing around and accidentally cut off landing crafts carrying the Scottish Essex on their way to the frontal attack, causing confusion and more delays. Finally, the Royal Regiment crafts head for Dieppe to fix their position and then change course for their landing site at Puits, to the east. The turbines surge as the small ships accelerate, heading toward shore with increased urgency. The noise is heard by the Germans in the harbour, who are waiting for one of their convoys to arrive in port. The enemy flashes for a recognition signal. The Canadian vessels carrying the Royal Regiment see the flashes and know they've been sighted. The Germans, not receiving the expected response, open fire. All inside the boats hold their breath as stray bullets ping against the armoured sides.

War correspondent Ross Munroe is on board one of these landing vessels. He adjusts his life belt and ducks down as best he can. There are 80 men in his landing craft and space is tight. He is nervously sitting on ammunition as bullets fly around him.

The firing ceases almost as soon as it starts, and the remaining 30 minutes pass peacefully. Still, the men duck lower and grip their guns in anticipation of the next blast, briefly wondering what it will be like to face the firing once the front doors have dropped open. In truth, it will be hell.

The element of surprise — so crucial to the mission — is now gone, and the Royals are hopelessly late in landing their men.

At 5:10 a.m., the landing crafts finally approach the beach near Puys. The sun is almost up, and tension is building in the dim dawning light of morning. German soldiers, watching the boats approach, man their gun positions along the cliffs and ignore the decoy planes above them. Suddenly, an enemy searchlight brightens the breaking day.

Speeding for shore, the landing crafts race to unload their men on the beach before the Germans on the cliffs begin shooting. In the lead, the men of the Royal Regiment's "B" Company sit in three rows facing the bow. Rifles are gripped with white knuckles, and each man urges the boat on faster as that damned searchlight illuminates the interior of the craft. Those sitting on the port and starboard sides are best protected from enemy gunfire, as the overhanging steel deck above their heads offers minimal shelter. But those sitting in the centre row are exposed to the guns above, with no protection except their helmets and their prayers.

Suddenly, the men's worst fears are realized as a rage of machine-gun fire from the cliff tops rakes the boat from stem to stern. Defenceless men scream in agony as their bodies are ripped apart. Their buddies, their comrades, can do nothing as blood splatters in all directions and then pools on the floor around their feet. The carnage increases as the boat mercilessly continues toward the shore — a shore with less protection for the men than the metal walls of the landing craft.

Amid men's screams and chattering guns, the hull scrapes the ocean bottom as it grinds to a halt. The bow ramp falls, and most of the men are felled where they sit. As the few survivors fight to get out of the boat, their boots slide on the blood of their dead or dying comrades. Those who are still able, climb over the bodies to make a rush for the door, only to come face to face with the hail of death from above. Bullets ricochet in all directions. The entire centre row is massacred.

The noise is horrific — a mind-numbing din of unbelievable proportions. High explosives burst on the shale along the shore, shattering the very air around the men. Machine-gun fire chatters, naval guns boom, sharp reports from field rifles penetrate the sound waves — all accompanied by the howling of aircraft engines and punctuated by the screams of the wounded and dying.

The survivors plunge into a metre of water as machine-gun rounds cut them down. The surf curls red foam around the feet of dead men still standing, until their bodies fall into the frigid water. The ramp is nearly impassable, as man after man is mowed down and body falls lifelessly on body. The living shove what's left of their comrades to one side and valiantly try to make it ashore. There is no other option.

Inside the boat, 20 of the 80 men are still alive. Making a group decision, they back the landing craft off the beach and try to reach the transport ships waiting offshore. Most of the survivors are badly wounded, and the medics on the landing boat are too poorly equipped to tend to them. The soldiers pull alongside an escort ship, leave their dead and wounded, then return to the battle.

Company Sergeant-Major MacIver sifts through the bodies in the water and makes his way to the beach. He sets his sights on the long stone wall at the foot of the cliff and mentally blocks out the massacre happening around him. As bullets kick at his feet, he hits the beach running for whatever protection the cliffs might offer. Suddenly, his head jerks back violently and he is knocked to his knees. His steel helmet is shattered from the bullet now lodged in his skull, below his right eye. The survival instinct kicks in. To stay where he is, is to die.

Struggling to his feet, he wipes the blood from his face. Beside him, his friend, Sergeant Tommy Preston of Vancouver, is hit. Falling to the ground, Tommy's leg spurts a fountain of blood where the enemy's bullets have all but severed it from the rest of his body. Forgetting himself, MacIver runs to help his friend. In the midst of the chaos, he grabs Tommy by the arms and lifts him onto his back. With a pathological indifference to enemy fire, he staggers up the stony beach with Tommy in tow. When he reaches the sea wall, MacIver loses consciousness and both men fall to the ground where the medics find them later and keep them safe until the evacuation boats arrive.

Meanwhile, Private Bill Stevens and Corporal Al MacDonald of "B" Company dive for the beach and are riddled with bullets. Crawling across the stretch of pebbled shore, they manage to drag themselves to the cliff face. Stevens is shot over 20 times, but hangs on to life and survives the battle.

As Private Stevens fights for his life, the landing craft carrying No. 16 Platoon falls short of the beach and the men plunge into over two metres of water. Many survive the hail of bullets from above only to drown — being pulled down by the heavy fighting gear. Private Jack Polton manages to reach the shore alive and wet, but without his rifle. Grabbing one from a dead comrade, he joins the battle.

In Private Steve Michell's boat, the entire centre row of men has been mowed down by the merciless firing from above. Climbing over and around the bodies, Private Michell fights to escape and reach the beach. As his boots slip on warm, sticky blood, he rolls one man aside and is shocked to find his platoon commander, Lieutenant Walters. The commander's assistant is also lying dead with his arms protectively over his officer's body. Blood is running in ribbons of red onto the floor and into the gutters of the boat. The hull is stained with it.

Private Michell is one of the lucky ones, managing to jump into chest-deep water. Wading ashore, rifle held above his head, he focuses on making it to the beach and then to the protection of the cliffs. Close to shore he finds his comrade, whose nickname in the regiment is "Smiler." The young man is still smiling as he stands quietly in the blood-red surf, struggling to stuff his own intestines back through the hole in his side. Whispering through contorted lips, the mortally wounded soldier tells Michell to make it out alive. Michell runs for the shelter of the cliff, hoping to find medical attention for Smiler, but the sight of all the ripped up humanity before him stops him in his tracks. Smiler had lied about his age to join the army, and now his young body floats lifelessly in the red of the Dieppe shore.

Only a dozen men remain from the 120 who originally made up "B" Company of the Royal Regiment of Canada. Out of the 100 of "A" Company, only 20 are still living. The bodies of the fallen carpet the slope to the cliff in layers. By the stone steps leading from the beach to the top of the cliffs, there are at least 60 lying dead, piled one on top of the other. Each surge of men trying to advance has to climb over the fallen, and then, as these men are cut down, the pile grows higher. Some, caught in the barbed wire, are left hanging in grotesque positions. Limbs, sheared off by the rain of bullets, lie bloody near dismembered torsos.

The commanding officer of the Royal Regiment, Lieutenant Colonel Douglas Catto, sails in to the beach at Puys a few moments later with the second wave of Canadian troops. Even from a distance, the massacre of his men is horrific. The colonel's bodyguard tries to convince his commander to call off the advance. The colonel refuses, saying he can't leave the dead and dying on a foreign beach. Besides, his orders are to advance at all costs.

As the second wave of troops hits the beach of death,

they are cut down like their comrades. Under fire from above, Privates Ronnie Reynolds and David Thistle set up a Bren gun and manically hammer at the German guns above them. Under cover of the Bren gun the Canadians again try to scale the sea wall.

The enemy, overly confident of victory, is out in the open now, running along the edge of the cliffs and dropping grenades on the men below. One of the grenades explodes between Reynolds and Thistle, wounding both men. Reynolds crawls back to the gun and grins as he squeezes off burst after burst at the pillbox on the cliff. Thistle is dragged out of the line of fire and taken to the medic station. He is later loaded onto a boat.

As Reynolds fires away, Private Freddy Corbett crawls back and forth, feeding the ammunition into the Bren. He's soon hit and can't go on. Another soldier crawls over, tucks the ammunition under one arm, and continues toward the Bren. Just three metres shy of his target, he is shot through the head. The ammunition finally runs out, and Reynolds has no choice but to retreat to the sea wall. The medics give him what medical aid they can, and he returns to the fighting.

On the western end of the beach, Lieutenant Colonel Catto has successfully landed with the Royals of "C" and "D" Companies. The Black Watch has also landed successfully, with mortars. The Canadians rally and the Germans get a taste of Canadian lead. The German soldiers concentrate their efforts on the new arrivals, and the mortar teams are soon slaughtered where they stand. However, during the shift of the enemy's attention, Lieutenant Colonel Catto and the remaining members of "C" and "D" Companies have time to reach the sea wall.

Lieutenant Bob Stewart stands up in full view of enemy machine guns and attacks, firing continuously from his Bren gun and providing cover for the wire-cutting team. The men work feverishly, and finally the wire springs loose. Catto and his men plunge through the gap in the wire and race up the hill. Stewart sinks to his knees, cradling his red-hot Bren gun, and grins. He's wounded seriously in the leg, but he got them through. It has only been an hour since they hit the beach.

With Catto leading them, the small group of advancing men burst into house after house, taking control as they go. Behind them, the enemy sends men to repair the hole in the barbed wire. Suddenly, the small group of attacking Canadians have the Germans in front of them and barbed wire at their backs. They fight gallantly, but they only number 14 against an army. With no way to rejoin their comrades, and running low on ammunition, those still alive hide in the nearby woods.

At 8 a.m., four hours after the men boarded the landing crafts, those still alive on the Puys beach are the first to surrender. The carnage on this small piece of shoreline is horrific, easily the highest casualties in the battle of Dieppe. As the survivors are being led away, the battles on the other beaches continue, heightening to a fevered pitch as the Canadian tenacity begins to crumble in the face of overpowering odds.

The main attack

The Reverend John W. Foote, honorary captain in the Canadian Army, is with his men waiting to board their landing crafts. A Presbyterian clergyman from Madoc, Ontario, Reverend Foote is chaplain of the Royal Hamilton Light Infantry (RHLI). He and the rest of the RHLI are part of the frontal attack on Dieppe. They are to land on the west end of the main beach, near an abandoned, war-ravaged casino. The Fusiliers Mont-Royal Regiment will follow.

At 4:15 a.m., Reverend Foote takes a deep breath. The call to board the landing boats reverberates throughout the ship. As he looks at the young faces around him, pale and eager in the grey light of dawn, the reverend tries not to think of those who will die in the fight ahead.

There is the muffled sound of shuffling feet as the men of the RHLI board the landing crafts. Using nets, they climb quietly over the sides of the big ships. One by one, they drop into the bobbing, square-nosed boats. Strict silence is the order, but sailors left behind on the ships' decks hoarsely whisper words of encouragement to the soldiers as they disappear over the sides.

Once the boats are loaded, they take to the waves, as the soldiers study the horizon uneasily. In the distance, flashes of tracer pierce the sky, while the heavy drone of approaching planes increases the tension of already taut nerves.

Suddenly, all hell breaks loose in the skies directly above Dieppe. British Hurricanes pepper the streets with tracer, while manoeuvering around buildings and drawing enemy guns away from the beach. Germans are running in all directions. The landing crafts draw closer to the shore, and the men crouch, praying the planes keep the enemy busy until they reach the cliffs.

The landing vessels nudge into the sand a few metres from shore and drop the doors. The men pour out into the surf and scramble to the beach, holding their guns at the ready. When the first wave of invaders hits the main beach, they fire their guns at the enemy posts, providing cover for those still in the water. The sound of the planes drowns out all other noise.

As the first few boats empty, others follow, spilling soldiers out of their innards with increased exigency. Waiting for their turn to disembark, soldiers on board the landing crafts watch in fascination as the enemy anti-aircraft guns growl and thud at the decoys. All thoughts of the beaches below the cliffs are forgotten by the Germans while their gunners follow the bombers inland, giving the invading soldiers that precious gift of time.

Soon, the guns of the Allied navy thunder from the Channel, and a protective smokescreen is laid down for the Canadians still unloading from the landing crafts. The convoy's destroyers fire hundreds of shells into the buildings along the front of the town. The Germans now have a battle on two fronts, and they crank their big guns back out to the sea.

The landing crafts awaiting their turn to disgorge their

passengers are caught in the middle of the ship to shore battle. Shells from the German guns hit the hydrogen bottles on board a few of the barges that are transporting tanks from the 14th Canadian Army Tank Division. There is smoke everywhere as flames leap into the dawn sky. Men screaming in pain leap overboard into the sea to douse the flames, only to drown — dragged to the ocean bottom by their heavy equipment. Others remain on board to face the raging fire. Among them is the crew that had befriended young Jim Still in England. As the little boy sleeps soundly in his bed, his Canadian friends are enmeshed in the fight of their lives.

Ed Bennett of Woodstock, Ontario, is one of the badly injured. Most of his clothing and battle dress are smoldering or have been blown off by the explosions. Seeing his buddies wounded around him, he acts on instinct and starts up his tank. The smell of his own burning flesh fills his nostrils as he lunges his mammoth equipment forward, driving it off the barge, into the water, through the waves, and onto the main beach. The icy salt water washes over his injuries, producing a pain so intense that he almost blacks out. Bile fills his throat as he pushes forward, driving his tank up and over the sea wall. It is the first tank to make it to the streets of Dieppe. Through the pain, Ed yells for the foot soldiers behind him to keep together and use him as a shield while he fires his mighty tank into the thick of the German defensive. He continues on until halted by a cement barricade. He is one of the few who survives his injuries.

Meanwhile, several squadrons of Hurricane bombers dive into the inferno on the ground. Lowering their landing gear to slow their approach for better aim, they fire repeatedly at Dieppe's main street and the Germans' rooftop guns. These brave pilots, fearless at low speeds and even lower altitudes, have a mission — to give cover to the infantry troops. In manic motion, the planes continue to fire into the streets and buildings, drawing the attention of the enemy up and away from the vulnerable men still in the water and along the shoreline.

John Mellor takes advantage of the cover and scrambles over the sea wall and into the street. Crouching and firing, he zigzags his way to the site of a German gun. Pulling a hand grenade from his pack, he throws it high, and it lands with a thud. He and his men fire a hail of bullets at the target as the grenade explodes, destroying the German gun. Then, following orders, he and his group fall back to the beach to offer cover for troops still landing.

Suddenly, there is a whiz past John's ear. As he turns to look for the source of the noise, a piece of shrapnel hits him, slicing through his skull and taking out one of his eyes. Dazed and confused, he finds himself climbing down over the cliff with the others. He looks at his blood-soaked shirt. His head feels like it's exploding, and he's sure he is dying. Hitting the beach running, he jumps into the sea to swim for England. A short time later, an escort boat picks him up and he's given medical aid. Eventually, he is transported back to England.

As a landing craft carrying a group of RHLI nears the beach, Bangalore torpedoes explode among the toggle ropes and grappling irons of the small boat. The platoon leader is blinded by the explosions and can only feel the water as it creeps up to his neck. Blinded for life, he and one other are the only survivors from the platoon who make it to shore.

Onshore, Reverend John Foote makes his way to a small, semi-sheltered hollow at the base of the cliff. Here, the regimental first-aid post for the RHLI has been set up. Shelling is intense as the Germans fire on the beach. Dirt is flying, men are screaming, and the din from the planes and flak is deafening. The wounded try to crawl to the medical station. Surrounded by whizzing bullets and exploding shells, the reverend remains on his feet. He ignores the threat to his own life and assists the medics, giving comfort to the wounded and dying as best he can.

A few metres away, a soldier runs from the waves to the base of the cliff. Guns blast from above and the man staggers and falls, shot again and again as he fights for survival. Struggling to his knees, the soldier begins crawling toward Reverend Foote, reaching out his hand before dropping to the ground. With dying and wounded all around, every available medic is occupied. John Foote grabs a first-aid kit and makes a mad dash, through flying bullets, to the injured man. He yells for assistance.

The stretcher party comes to the reverend's aid and transports the soldier to the first-aid post. All the way to the post, the chaplain stays beside the suffering man, giving him strength and courage, gripping his hand tightly until they are safe.

The bitter battle rages on. Pinned by the shore batteries, many men never make it out of the water. Their lifeless bodies roll back and forth in the surf. By mid-morning, the officers in the first-aid post decide to move to the cover of a landing craft, which has been left high and dry by the receding tide. They carry the casualties to the new refuge. Reverend Foote is one of the first to move out with the stretcher-bearers, holding the hands of the wounded and ignoring the whiz of bullets around them. Time after time, he makes the trip through enemy fire. Above the booming, he shouts words of encouragement, giving strength not only to those on the stretchers, but also to the unarmed medics.

Finally, the boats arrive to evacuate the survivors. One by one, the wounded are helped out to the boats while bullets ricochet around them. The medics run back and forth with the stretchers, dodging gunfire as best they can.

Not all of the landing boats can make it back to shore. Some are stranded by the receding tide, and space is limited along the beach. There are more men than available seats in the crafts. The men still on shore valiantly provide cover for the retreating troops. They fight on, matching the Germans shot for shot until their ammunition is spent.

Helping a man into the last landing craft to leave the beach, Reverend Foote is pulled into the boat by a couple of the retreating soldiers. A few metres offshore, he leaps over the side and back into the water, shouting over his shoulder, "The men left behind need me more than the ones on the ships."

Finally, in late afternoon, with their ammunition gone and their injured needing more medical help than what they can provide, the Canadians left in Dieppe lift their arms and surrender to the enemy. Among the remaining troops is Reverend Foote, who is taken prisoner with his fellow Canadians. He continues to minister to them as a POW.

* * *

The flotilla limps helplessly back to England with her survivors. All ships return but one, the HMS *Calpe* with General Roberts onboard.

Bringing the destroyer as close to shore as possible, Roberts wants to ensure that all the men who could be saved were picked up. And so, with bullets ricocheting off the metal hull in dull staccato notes, the crew of the *Calpe* searches for survivors. A few men clinging to wreckage in the water are hoisted on board. Then this ship, too, turns for home.

By noon on August 19, all of the survivors who can be pulled off the beaches around Dieppe are safely at sea. After only eight hours, the fight is over, and those left behind watch as their ships disappear over the horizon, heading for England. The Allied planes bank over the town of Dieppe and also head for home, firing off a couple of rounds. The receding sound of their throbbing engines call for the German guns to fall silent. The mechanical din diminishes, as do the sounds of gunfire. The cliffs now echo with the sound of the waves, and the moans of dying and wounded men.

On one side of the main beach, a lone soldier is impossibly tangled in a coil of barbed wire. Wounded and struggling to escape, he yanks the wire with bare hands and screams as the steel rips through his bruised flesh. His whimpers and pleadings for help are silenced when an enemy machine gun cuts him down. His body jerks with the impact of the bullets, then quivers as the life pours out of his body in a river of red, soaking the pebbles at his feet. In slow motion, he falls forward onto the sand as his fellow Canadian soldiers watch silently — helplessly — beyond grief.

By the end of the raid on Dieppe, 907 of the 5000 Canadians involved lie dead or dying on those beaches, and another 1000 are wounded. More than 1940 survive the war in prisoner of war camps. Only 2210 make it back to England.

To their family, friends, and comrades, and to young boys such as Jim Still, the Canadians who fought at Dieppe were real people, not simply numbers. And whether our soldiers were decorated or not, whether they returned home or died in obscurity, each and every one of them should be remembered "for matchless gallantry." For the battle of Dieppe was not lost due to cowardice or a weakness of spirit; it was lost because dead men can no longer fight.

Chapter 3
Memories of Italy

G host ships, they seem to be. Only the splashing of the waves and the shadowy outline of their hulls reveal their presence in the pre-dawn darkness off the coast of Sicily. It is July 10, 1943, and there are nearly 3000 Allied troopships, landing crafts, and warships gathering for the invasion of Sicily and the big push to Rome — then onward.

The ships are in blackout conditions; all hatches and portholes are blocked against escaping light. Down below, the lights are a dim blue. In one ship, Corporal Norton is patiently making small cuts in his web belt for his .303 ammunition. Meanwhile, Burgoone, a Bren gunner, is trying out a can of self-heating soup. He lights a fuel pellet in the bottom of the soup tin and the liquid in the top heats up quickly — a nice change from the regular army staples of hardtack and bully beef. Elsewhere, men are dressing for combat, writing letters home, and poring over the battle plans.

On all the ships there's a short interdenominational service at 11 p.m. Many of the men have already taken part in a service that morning. However, this doesn't stop them from turning out for the later one as well.

After the service, some stay and chat, while others go to their quarters for final preparations. Slim Liddell's men are in their cabins, stripped to the waist and blackening their faces and arms with a charcoal paste made from burned paper. Slim firmly believes that this camouflage will help hide them from the enemy.

Nearby, Private Fred Snell of Stony Mountain, Manitoba, is in his own cabin, putting together his pack and trying in vain to lighten his load. He will be one of the last men to disembark, bringing up the rear on a motorbike. His job is to herd those falling behind and keep the line moving. The back of the line may seem like a cushy place to be, but wounded enemy soldiers become snipers, and nowhere on the battlefield is there a truly safe position.

In the next cabin, face-blackened Captain Len Carling is struggling with heavy battle webbing. Wrapped around the body, this reinforced steel material is cumbersome, but worth every ounce in protection. Len has already loaded his machine gun, and his pack is filled with additional ammunition, grenades, a folding shovel, personal belongings, and two days' worth of rations. There are no Allied restaurants, hotels, or corner stores where the men are going. Supplies will be run up the line by truck, motorbike, and on the backs of animals, but if the Germans bomb the supplies, rations will be vital.

Many of the men have been at sea in cramped quarters for days and are out of shape from the lack of exercise. The first few days of marching will be hard on them, especially with the added 31 kilograms each will carry.

In the early morning hours, the order echoes through the ships. Each section, identified by number, is to report to the boat stations immediately. The waiting is over and daily life is about to change drastically.

Strangely silent, the men file out into the corridors, each of them grasping the bayonet scabbard of the man ahead to keep the line intact. Moving in unison, they shuffle slowly up the companionways to the decks above — left, right, left, right. The chatter of anti-aircraft guns on shore accompanies their progress as the enemy attempts to defend its claim to the island of Sicily.

The soldiers board the transport boats; 35 to 40 men take up cramped and crouching positions in three rows, in some cases spooning in order to fit everyone into the small vessels. Packed in tightly, they watch as the boats to their left and right are bumped and lowered, tilting this way and that, until each is dropped into the waves below. On the way down, one boat bumps up against the hull of a ship at the same time that bilge water pours out of the drainage spout. The soldiers in the boat are drenched in the stinking mess. As the men choke and cough, the craft drops, hits the water, and is then pulled back and forth by the waves until it's released from the ship's line.

"Welcome to Italy," someone mutters.

In the rough sea, the small boats roll constantly and many soldiers lose the contents of their stomachs. Once one person begins to vomit, others quickly follow, and soon the sides of the boats are dotted with the heads of sick soldiers as the vessels continue to pitch up and down, back and forth.

As the landing crafts hit the beach, the Canadian navy behind them open fire on the coastal targets, and bullets whiz above the boats. The skies over the island light up as the cacophony of exploding shells fills everyone's ears. Dawn is lightening the skies to the music of battle.

"Down doors!"

The order is shouted above the sound of machine guns spitting from the 15 pillboxes ringing the shore. Spilling from the guts of the vessels, the men plunge into the frigid, waist-deep seawater. The waves drag at the heavy battle dress, and the soldiers, gripping their guns with white knuckles, struggle to stay on their feet.

Splashing onto the beach, the first line of troops crouches and fires at the enemy guns. Meanwhile, the second wave of men overtakes the first and, moving forward, snips barbed wire with wire cutters. The guns on the boats offshore make short work of the enemy's token resistance, while soldiers pour through the holes in the wire.

The 1st Canadian Infantry Brigade, including the Royal Canadian Regiment, the Hastings and Prince Edward Regiment, and the 48th Highlanders, lands on the right side of the beach. Surging ahead on the left side of the beach is the 2nd Infantry Brigade, including the Seaforth Highlanders of Canada and the Princess Patricia's Canadian Light Infantry (PPCLI). The Loyal Edmonton Regiment brings up the rear, with motorcycles weaving back and forth behind the advancing troops. Private Fred Snell is on one of these bikes.

The forward observing officers, called "fooers," have already jumped in from aircraft and surveyed the area for mines. They are quickly travelling inland to report enemy movements. Other fooers are brought in by gliders towed by Dakota aircraft. Poor navigation causes the early release of the gliders too far out to sea, and many aboard are drowned. Those who land successfully press inland.

By 8 a.m., tanks, guns, Bren-gun carriers, and trucks are rolling north as the air force circles above. Back on the beach, supply ships are unloading their precious cargo, and trucks are moving out to follow the army.

Thirty metres above the high-tide mark, Roger Beach connects to a low ridge of limestone, only three metres high and topped with sand dunes perfectly packed for vehicle travel (for once, advance intelligence is right.) About a kilometre inland, the soldiers head down a narrow dirt path to the junction of a major road where the airfield is located. The airfield is quickly secured.

One of the first fooers to this point is Sergeant Louis Therian, from northwestern Ontario. His father had been a railroad man, and Louis grew up in the country, without electricity, running water, or indoor plumbing. Louis learned to hunt as soon as he could lift a gun, and tracked game in every season, on every type of terrain. To him, survival is a way of life and he can read signs in the grass that escape the eyes of most men. He is part of what the army refer to as "Combined Ops." He's trained in artillery, infantry, and paratrooping. He is with the 8th Army, under Field Marshal Bernard L. Montgomery.

After landing more or less uneventfully on the beach, the Canadians travel inland for about five days before encountering German fire just outside the village of Grammichele. Once inland, the Canadian troops are at a disadvantage. The retreating Italian and German armies have already been over the ground and are familiar with the area. At first, they leave in a hurry, and the invading troops make good time. Later, closer to the Gustav and Hitler Lines, the Germans shell the roads behind them, destroying the bridges, and burning the crops. Fresh water becomes a luxury to the advancing army, and supplementing their rations with local fresh produce becomes difficult.

As fooers, Louis and his small group of men go ahead of the main push and travel level with the enemy line. They seek out the enemy strongholds and radio the information back to the commanding officer. When strategically possible, Louis orders firing to commence from the artillery, using coordinates in code terms such as "bubble-line bubble-line bubble."

Each time, the procedure is the same. Initially, Louis gives the coordinates of a location a little past the target so the first shell will overshoot the enemy. One gun takes aim and fires. Louis watches where the shell lands and then sends the adjusted coordinates back to the artillery so the second shell will fall short in order to pinpoint the location somewhere in the middle. They fire again, and the fooer adjusts the third set of coordinates. If luck is with them, the third shot falls in between the first two and right in the middle of the enemy ranks. Because of this method, fooers are often directly in the line of fire from their own guns, and casualties from friendly fire are not uncommon.

Fooers travel best under the cover of darkness, and one night in Sicily is especially black. The rain falls in a silent drizzle, blocking out the stars. The fooers are parallel with the enemy, and the lack of light has everyone alert for the slightest sound. Somewhere out there are the Turkish soldiers. Though they are fighting on the Allies' side, the Turks nevertheless give Louis the shivers. They keep to themselves and move about like silent shadows — presences felt but unseen.

Louis thinks he hears a noise and crouches by a tree. It's so dark; visibility is almost zero. He is silent and hardly breathing as he listens. Suddenly, an arm comes up behind him and he feels cold steel against his throat. He is forced back against the tree so hard that the bark is biting into his back. His assailant's other hand pats his shoulder, locating the Canadian Army crest there. Then the hand moves to Louis's boots and feels for the way the laces are tied. In a flash, the knife is gone, and so is the hand that held it. It is almost as if Louis dreamed the whole thing. That is how the Turks identify the Canadians — by the crest on the shoulder and the way their boots are laced.

The rest of the men in the army are suffering their own troubles. Private Clarence Murphy is with the Carleton and York Regiment (part of the 3rd Infantry Brigade). He has marched the first nine days into Sicily without even unlacing his boots. When rest is finally called, Murphy finds his socks worn through, leaving raw, bleeding, and infected sores. He cleans them up as best he can and wraps a field bandage around his feet in order to continue the march. The infantry waits for no man.

Along with blisters and aching muscles from the constant travelling, the men are suffering from large sores on their exposed skin, caused by continuous exposure to the elements. Many wake up during the night from the pain. They squeeze the boils until they burst, and then go back to sleep. Murphy's platoon leader tells the men to put urine on their sores and they'll go away. Many follow his advice, and find that he is right.

Fresh water is scarce at the front. The weather is hot during the day and cold at night. The small creeks are few and far between, muddy and filled with soap from the hundreds of bodies that have already bathed in them. Toilets are where the soldiers make them, but without wash water, dysentery becomes a debilitating problem. One soldier asks his platoon leader if they can postpone the war on account of the runs.

The Canadians march and fight their way up the Italian boot for months — from Calabria to the Foggia Plain, and then to Ortona.

* * *

Ortona, Italy. Dark and cold, the icy winds blow over the hills and down into the gullies, howling like a lonely wolf. Christmas 1943 is only weeks away, and sheets of sleet and rain hammer at the buildings — and at the Canadians approaching the outskirts of the town. These men, cold and homesick, have orders to take Ortona, which is not going to be easy. The city is almost empty of civilians. Whoever was left after the Germans snatched all the able-bodied men for slave labour, fled to escape Hitler's tyranny.

Two battalions of German paratroopers are all that stand between Ortona and the invading forces. Knowing they will be outnumbered, the Germans use everything at their disposal to even the odds. They sink ships to block the harbour and barricade the streets and alleys with garbage, rubble, and old cars. Only the main street remains open, to channel Canadian attackers into the heavily mined town's square, where the defenders are planning to ambush with snipers, mortars, and anti-tank guns. It's a fine welcome to the bone-weary soldiers so far away from their homes and families during the festive season.

Acting Major Paul Triquet, from Cabano, Quebec, with the Royal 22nd Regiment, sits down with Major H. A. Smith from the "C" Squadron of the Canadian Armoured Division to plan the attack. The two spread out an army map pinpointing the port of Ortona on the Adriatic Sea. This is one of their objectives. Another is the crossroads located approximately one kilometre northeast of the hamlet of Casa Berardi, for if German reinforcements arrive, they will have to travel down that road. Holding these two points is paramount to winning Ortona.

At 7:30 a.m. on December 11, the company of the Royal 22nd sets out for the crossroads, battling through booby-trapped fields and mine-infested olive groves. Later that morning, as the men approach the gully on their way to Casa Berardi, a barrage of enemy guns suddenly shatters the morning quiet. Shells screech overhead and plough into the earth, spraying up dirt, shrapnel, and smoke. Men scream as they fall to the ground. It's apparent that the enemy is holding the area with strength, and that Captain Triquet's men are outnumbered and outgunned.

Captain Triquet shouts his orders through the din and smoke, telling his men not to panic. The men dive for cover, dragging their wounded to safety whenever possible. Private Otto Wuerch of Winnipeg, Manitoba, runs to find refuge in a nearby church with a group of others. The bombing and shelling intensify, and the Canadians rush up to the front of the church and crouch behind a large wooden cross. Shell after shell rocks the walls around them, loosening the ancient mortar and sending large chunks of stone crashing to the floor in clouds of lung-choking dust. When the roof collapses, all but the cross turns to rubble. After the attack ends, none of the men behind the cross is injured.

Meanwhile, a fooer radios the map coordinates to the Canadian Army, who open fire with everything they have. A six-man crew has their made-in-Canada guns firing in seconds from up to 11 kilometres away. In answer to the Germans' attack, 25-pound howitzer shells fly overhead. One by one, the enemy guns are silenced, and the first German outpost is captured — but not before the fooer is killed.

The casualties are high. All of the company officers and 50 percent of the men are killed or wounded. The wounded are carried to deserted farmhouses. Captain Triquet surveys the damage and reorganizes his troops. Signalling for Major Smith's tanks, what's left of the infantry falls in behind the mighty metal monsters, and the forward push continues.

But the enemy hasn't given up. Before the Canadians get far down the road, a roar of enemy tanks is heard. Two

German tanks descend on them from a gully below the road, while a third begins to fire on the Allies from behind a farmhouse, trapping them in the crossfire.

The infantry leap off the road and into the shelter of a ravine, leaving Major Smith's tanks to handle the battle. The air above the men is thick with bullets. Shells burst around them, hailing down earth and debris.

On the road, the fight is on. The Allied tanks fire; the ground trembles. Two German tanks fire back, while the third finds shelter in some trees. Captain Triquet sends a wireless message requesting artillery support, giving coordinates "bubble-line, bubble-line, zero." Within minutes, shells whistle overhead and trees explode. The German tanks retreat, leaving the way clear.

With the enemy in check, the Allied tanks lead the way along a narrow trail that the Canadians have nicknamed "the Lager track." An easier route for the tanks than the more direct route from San Leonardo, this trail skirts the gully and joins the Ortona road.

A few minutes after noon on December 11, only about a quarter of the 80 men originally in Captain Triquet's company of Royal 22nd soldiers are able to continue. Finally in sight of the crossroads, which is still being held by the Germans, the last remnants of Triquet's company are ordered to hold their position at all costs.

The reserves are called in, and the West Nova Scotia Regiment pushes through the Seaforth Highlanders' positions, capturing the lateral road in the vicinity of Casa Berardi. The Germans are well dug in, and very little artillery support is possible for the Canadians. The attack fails miserably.

The Germans aggressively close in on the Canadians, but Major Smith's tanks form a wagon-train circle, and the Canadians dig in. They continue the fight. Reinforcements reach them at nightfall and the battle rages all through the night.

At 8 a.m., the Canadians attack once more. They must gain control of the crossroads. The Germans of the 1st Battalion of the 200th Panzer Grenadier Regiment hit them with everything they have. Shells whistle, bullets whiz from both sides, and explosions send rocks and splinters of wood flying in all directions. The battle continues all day. Periodically, the smoke and debris block out the sun, making it hard to guess the time of day.

The Canadians' wireless is knocked out again and again. The Germans launch four counterattacks against the Canadians. The Canadians hold fast. Eager to close in on the enemy, the army's forward soldiers crawl from their slit-trenches to the crest of the gully. Intense machine-gun fire meets their advance, and casualties mount. The commanding officer, Lieutenant Colonel M. P. Bogert of the West Nova Scotia Regiment, is wounded but continues to direct the battle until he is relieved in the early afternoon. The deadly stalemate persists, with high body counts on both sides. Neither side is giving an inch, matching shell for shell, shot for shot, death for death.

By the night of December 12, reinforcements have strengthened both sides. Much needed food is brought in for the Canadians — the first that many of the men have tasted in two days. Their spirits are rejuvenated, and on the morning of the 13th, the Canadians rush forward. Leading the front line, Triquet yells for his 14 remaining men. Back-up shelling is ordered, and the tanks rumble to life.

The Germans, also refreshed, meet the challenge head-on, throwing everything they have at the Canadians. The battle becomes personal, no longer one country and army against another. It is man-to-man, hand-to-hand, as the two sides collide with deafening screams and shelling from overhead. Smoke fills the air; shrapnel finds soft flesh, and the acrid stench of cordite mixes with the odour of burning bodies.

Fooer Louis Therian is off to one side of the main unit, slipping through the trees as silently as a ghost. He stops for a second, listening, but besides the sounds of the battle around him, he hears nothing.

Suddenly, the hair on the back of his neck stands on end and he senses the threat before the German strikes from behind the trees. Louis jumps back and sideways, but too late. There's a burning in his thigh as a bayonet digs deeply, impaling the bone. He gasps and reaches for his knife. The German discharges his rifle into Louis's leg in order to withdraw the bayonet, then poises for the next thrust. Blood spurts from Louis's wound, but there is no time for pain. The German is intent on finishing him off.

Louis rolls as he falls free of the bayonet and kicks the enemy's feet out from under him. The German grunts as he lands hard. Jumping on top of him, Louis grabs the man's hair and slits his throat. Feeling the warmth flow over his hand and hearing the gurgling as the man dies, Louis lets the body go. He rips some material off the German's undershirt and stuffs it in the hole in his thigh, which is big enough to put his fist into. Blood runs down his leg and fills his boot. He ties his belt tightly around the wound to stem the flow and, after a moment, moves on. The battle isn't over.

The Canadians manage to clean out three machine-gun nests on their side of the gully and take 21 prisoners. But the Germans' murderous machine-gun and mortar fire wreak havoc on all who show their heads above the crest of the gully. Those not cut down must retreat to a safer distance. Low cloud cover prevents fighter and bomber support. The tanks and the men fight alone. On December 19, they have taken the area, setting up headquarters in a ruined farmhouse.

The Germans launch attack after attack on the farmhouse, and the ground vibrates with the shelling from both sides. But the men of the Royal 22nd Regiment stand firm. Captain Triquet yells out to his men, "*Ils ne passeront pas!*" (They shall not pass.) And the Canadians throw themselves even more vigorously into the battle.

A group stays at the crossroads, while the rest of the Canadian Army and Allies push on to Ortona. The Germans do not pass.

Soon, Louis Therian is able to find a medic at a Regimental Aid Post. His wound is still bleeding freely and requires more attention than he has time for. With jeep ambulances transporting the more seriously wounded, and with the gruesome task of burying the dead, the medics are kept busy. Nonetheless, they find the time to administer luxuries many of the men haven't enjoyed for days: a cup of tea, a can of insect powder, fresh fruit, biscuits, news, and a friendly face. An hour after Louis is re-bandaged, he's back on the front, carrying extra bandages. Wounded or not, there is still a battle to be fought and a war to win. Only the very seriously wounded will be sent home; the rest will carry on.

The Canadians begin their main attack on Ortona at noon on December 20. The first push into town is led by the Loyal Edmonton Regiment and supported by the Sherman tanks of the Three Rivers Regiment and the Saskatoon Light Infantry, along with the Ninetieth Anti-Tank Battery.

Located on the coast of the Adriatic, the town of Ortona was established during medieval days, when the maritime power of Venice dominated the shipping trades. The town's focal point is a massive 15th century castle with a high promontory projecting into the sea. Around this imposing stone structure huddles the town itself, where narrow streets and wall-to-wall houses make it almost impossible for tank and troop movement — perfect for an ambush. To make matters worse, the eastern edge of the town borders a precipitous cliff that falls away to the small, artificial harbour, enclosed by a pair of breakwaters. A deep ravine west of Ortona restricts the townsite to an average width of 455 metres. This also limits the invading troops. Ortona is virtually impregnable on three sides, making it easy to defend, and almost impossible to overcome. The small group of German paratroopers have all the cards stacked in their favour. The Canadians will have to devise a new way of waging war in order to take the town.

On December 21, the battle transforms into hand-to-hand and house-to-house combat. The fighting is so fierce that the infantry are pinned inside buildings by the heavy machine-gun fire and resort to "mouse-holing": chopping through the walls of one house, they gain access to the house next door. When that house has been taken, they chop through to the next, flushing out enemy soldiers as they find them and remaining unexposed to the streets lined with snipers.

The Allied advance is finally halted on the brink of a minefield near the town square. The engineers rush forward to clear it so the tanks can proceed, but they are soon pinned down by enemy fire. There isn't enough cover for the men, and the situation is desperate. Sergeant George Campion, a Métis soldier from Tofield, Alberta, grabs a pocketful of smoke grenades. Running 10 metres through the minefield and into an open street, he throws the grenades, laying a smokescreen as cover for the engineers. He then runs back to his platoon for more grenades. His buddies hold their breath as he zigzags to dodge bullets and avoid land mines.

Back and forth he travels, gathering more smoke grenades to maintain the smokescreen. Puffs of dirt leap around his feet as the Germans keep firing, and yet he is unharmed. Thanks to Sergeant Campion, the minefield is cleared and the army moves forward.

The fighting continues, and December 25 arrives. Christmas in Ortona is unlike any Christmas the Canadian soldiers have experienced. Nothing looks, smells, or tastes like the holiday season. Instead, rubble, smoke, cordite, and dust greet the senses. The enemy attacks tirelessly the entire day in what is described by CBC correspondent Matthew Halton as "a carnival of fury."

Still, battalion administrative personnel are determined that, whatever the situation, their rifle companies should at the very least have a Christmas dinner.

The place for the Seaforths' banquet is the abandoned Church of Santa Maria di Constantinopoli. The main room is set with long rows of tables adorned with white tablecloths. Somehow, the organizers are able to provide each man with a bottle of beer, as well as candies, cigarettes, nuts, fruit, and chocolate bars. The commanding officer, Lieutenant Colonel S. W. Thomson, orders the companies to eat in relays. While one small group enjoys a meal of soup, pork with applesauce, mixed vegetables, mashed potatoes, gravy, Christmas pudding, and mince pie, the rest of the men continue fighting in the streets. Then, once that group finishes their meal, they are replaced with a new group of men.

The looks on the faces of the war-weary soldiers are ones of disbelief as they file in and sit down at decorated tables. Wearing the same mud-soaked clothing they've worn for the last 30 days, these men eat their festive meal and listen to "Silent Night," well aware that their comrades are battling for their lives only metres away. Minutes later, they are replaced by yet another group of men.

For some, this Christmas dinner is their last meal.

Casualties mount on both sides until December 28, when Ortona falls into Allied hands. The blood of soldiers soaks the ground, baptizing the coastal town. After burying their dead, several Canadians solemnly march to the entrance of the town and erect a sign in memory of their fallen comrades. It reads: THIS IS ORTONA — A WESTERN CANADIAN TOWN.

Chapter 4
The Push
for Freedom

The haze hanging over the Liri Valley on May 23, 1944, is thick. The men are soaked by it, and their eyes are strained trying to see through it. Their orders are simple: breach the Hitler Line. The job is necessary, but almost impossible. As determined as the Canadian soldiers are to succeed, the enemy is just as determined to keep the advancing army from breaking through the line.

As the Seaforth Highlanders, Princess Patricia's Canadian Light Infantry, and others move carefully and quickly through a stand of oak trees, the enemy opens fire with everything it has. At first, the Patricia's on the extreme right forge ahead, closing in on the Germans' second of five report lines. Meanwhile, the North Irish Horse tanks roll forward, flattening everything in their way. The ground trembles as they pass.

Kaboom! Rat-tat-tat! The tanks find a minefield. Breathing is laboured as cordite-laden smoke fills the senses and hangs heavily in the air. *Kaboom!* There's screaming as a tank rolls over another mine. The vehicle's top hatch flies open, and flames leap skyward. Men, covered in burning fuel with flesh dripping off them, crawl out of the top of the blazing tank and lie helplessly on the hot metal, knowing they are dying and powerless to prevent it. No one can get near enough to help — although there's no hope for the men anyway. Their lungs are charred, their eyes are burned, and their skin is blackened beyond recognition. Their bodies fry like eggs. For those still living, all the onlookers can do is wait until the agony passes, knowing the cries of their friends will haunt their dreams for the rest of their lives. They pray the end comes quickly. In total, 44 disabled tanks litter the area by the end of the battle.

Along the edges of the minefield the bushes come to life, as camouflaged Panther tanks swivel their branch-laden guns, taking aim at the Patricias and the North Irish tank units. The Canadians fall back, and the Allied troops fight their way into the dubious cover of a nearby gully, which branches off from the main Forme Valley along the Hitler Line. The two leading companies of the Patricias and the Seaforths spread out. They dig in to wait out the worst of the enemy's attack and hold their positions until reinforcements arrive. The rest of the army is scattered; the Germans have successfully fragmented the organization of the invaders. Platoons and small groups of men have been separated. Radios are useless, fighting is fierce, and each group is on its own.

Private Fred Snell's small platoon of Patricias digs in. The platoon leader, Captain Wilson, tells everyone to keep low, stay calm, and make every shot count. They only number about 22. Huddling in their slit trenches on the outskirts of an open field that contains land mines, they await nightfall.

Fred is working closely with Captain Wilson, who is dressed in regular private's battle dress with a helmet. This is to ensure that snipers looking for an officer to pick off will have a hard time differentiating him from the rest of the men. Fred, meanwhile, is wearing an officer's beret. He is aware that snipers will probably mistake him for the platoon leader, but part of his job is to ensure the safety of his officer.

The platoon is waiting for tanks and reinforcements, or at least radio contact. They can only guess at the location of the other Canadians and the rest of the army. The telegrapher tries to send a message on the wireless. So far, nothing is working.

Opposite the clearing is a small stand of trees. With the pre-dusk light comes a popping sound. Snipers, well hidden in the foliage, begin picking off the Canadians one by one. Some of the Patricias slump forward in the muck, eyes open but unseeing, while others fire back into the trees. *Rat-tat-tat* — a yell down the line and the sound of returning fire. Men are falling, and the snipers keep shooting. Blood begins to fill the bottom of the small trench, and several Patricias are wrapping their own wounds with field dressings they have stored inside their helmets.

Fred Snell is crouched next to his platoon leader when a sniper bullet hits Captain Wilson in the neck, and he falls across Fred's knee. The captain struggles to breathe, choking on his own blood. Fred tries to staunch the blood pumping from Wilson's neck wound and yells for a medic. No one comes. Fred keeps his hand on the wound, but the blood seeps through his fingers and down his leg. In seconds his leader is dead, so Fred gently places him in the bottom of the trench.

Looking around, Fred sees other members of his platoon shot and bleeding. Seven men in all lay dead or dying at the bottom of the slimy trench. The snipers are beyond grenade range; they have the Canadians pinned.

Unwilling to watch helplessly, Fred begins to run up and down the lines, rallying the surviving men to fight back. He shouts encouragement and orders the men to silence the enemy guns. Then, in shock, and without thought for his personal safety, Fred grabs his machine gun and calmly walks out into the minefield. Standing in the open, he surveys the area, looking high in the trees for anything that seems like it doesn't belong — a branch out of place, a movement, or something that doesn't quite fit.

A branch in a tree to his right catches his eye. Steadily,

he lifts his machine gun and fires a short burst. A man falls to the ground in a flurry of fluttering leaves and broken branches. Then Fred hears another popping sound to his left, and a movement draws his attention. He rolls to the ground instinctively and comes up on one knee. A bullet whizzes past his ear. He takes a deep breath, aims his gun at the trees, and fires another round. A second sniper hits the ground. Fred, thinking there are no more, begins to return to his men. A sound stops him short. Turning quickly and crouching, he fires on instinct. A third sniper is killed.

Fred Snell takes over leading the small group of men until they safely join the rest of their company. Before the war is over, he is wounded three times in Italy — the final injury, along with malaria, sends him home.

Chapter 5
Smokey Smith Earns his Title

he nights are dark, wet, and miserable. The October mornings roll in thick with fog, and once the mist gives the men a good soaking, the rain sets in — day after day. No soldier has dry feet, and each man is wearing all the clothing he possesses in order to stay warm. They are muddy and chilled to the bone. Sitting around charcoal fires that smoulder in biscuit tins or old oilcans only adds to their desolation. The greyness around them makes them homesick and anxious.

There's a shortage of food, ammunition, and dry everything. There haven't been any supplies delivered in over a week; either the Germans have bombed the supply trucks, or the soldiers are moving too fast for the trucks to catch up. Whatever the reason, the Canadians have to search the countryside for edible bark, berries, roots, wild onions — whatever can be thrown into a big pot and served hot when their schedule and the Germans permit, or cold when they don't.

The fooers have it worse than the others. Moving silently behind enemy lines, Louis Therian has gone without food for three days. Hungry, he lets himself into a small lean-to on the side of an abandoned farmhouse. To his joy, he finds a bun made of Italian bread. It's so old and hard it almost breaks his teeth, but he doesn't care. To him, it's the most delicious meal he's ever eaten, and one he will never forget.

So far in Italy, the Canadians have lost 2400 — they have been killed, wounded, or taken prisoner. Over 1600 soldiers are sick.

It is October 1944, and the men of the Seaforth Highlanders, along with their comrades in the Princess Patricia's Canadian Light Infantry, are in the Italian town of Cesena, a few kilometres from the shores of the Adriatic Sea. They are pushing through the town and out across the bridge over the Savio River — a German stronghold. Morale is low; Canadian Thanksgiving has passed, and the troops are tired of being in a foreign place, fighting an uphill battle. They want this war to end.

A group of Patricias storms the bridge, dodging, crouching, firing, rolling — determined to overrun the enemy and push onward. The German machine guns bark to life, mowing the Canadians down, killing some and wounding others. The enemy is also determined — determined to drive the

Canadians all the way back to Canada, if possible.

The rest of the Canadian soldiers are holed up in a nearby church. They barely have enough time to camouflage the Hawkins grenades and get the Projector, Infantry, Anti-Tank guns (PIATs) in place before the Germans have them pinned down.

Darkness comes early, and soon after the sun disappears, rain begins falling again. The Allied force is waiting for the right moment to launch another offensive to cross the bridge. Suddenly, they hear the rumbling of German tanks approaching the other side of the bridge. The Canadians steel themselves for a bitter battle.

Three lone Seaforth Highlanders — members of the anti-tank platoon — slide down the muddy bank of the river and into the water, holding their guns and ammunition above their heads. If the Germans break through into town, the fighting will get even uglier. The tanks have to be taken out, whatever the cost.

The water is waist-deep and cold, and the rushing current at the centre of the river almost sweeps the three Canadians away. Their feet slip on the slimy stones of the river bottom, and they suffer more of a dunking than they bargained for. Thinking they have reached the height of misery, they arrive on the other side only to find that the bank there is four metres high and twice as muddy as the one they had slid down. They climb carefully — as the Germans have mined the banks — slipping and slogging through the mud in an impossible uphill path.

Once they gain the top, Private Ernest Alvia Smith, a 29-year-old from New Westminster, British Columbia, and his two companions set up their special anti-tank guns close to the bridge's entrance, off to one side by some bushes. Across the bridge, "C" Company is under heavy fire from the Germans, and judging the direction of the attack, the small group of three thinks they are ready for whatever the Germans have in mind.

Through the *rat-tat-tat* and thudding of the guns from both sides, the three men listen for the drone of the three German Panther tanks descending on the bridge. As expected, the tanks are led by a German staff car filled with officers, as well as two large guns on tracks. However, following this entourage are 30 foot soldiers bringing up the rear.

Smith and his companions look at each other and gulp. Realizing they are in the direct path of these mammoth metal monsters, and that the force is greater than anticipated, they decide to change their position. They grab their weapons and ammunition and make a mad dash across the field and road. Before they reach the ditch on the other side, a third tank (Mark V) lumbers down the road and sweeps the area with its machine guns, wounding one of the three Canadians in the arm. In full view of the enemy, Smith fires his anti-tank gun. The shell explodes, stopping the Mark V in its tracks and giving Smith time to help his wounded comrade carry his gun and ammo to the new location in the ditch across the road.

Back across the river, the trio's platoon provides as much cover for them as possible. However, it is also under heavy fire from the same Germans.

As bullets whiz past them from all directions, the three men quickly set up and take aim at the enemy. Trying their best to ignore the puffing dust at their feet, they begin firing — if they let this group over the bridge, a bloodbath will follow and Cesena will fall back into enemy hands.

Behind the tanks, 10 German foot soldiers rush to arm the guns and take a bead on the three men who are firing machine pistols and throwing grenades. Smith and his men bravely stand their ground. The tanks are almost on top of them now, and the Germans outnumber them at least 12 to 1. The Germans crank their guns around. *Whumph!* The shot is too far, landing behind the three men with an earth-shattering explosion. Dirt rains from above, and the smell of gunpowder fills the trio's nostrils. *Whumph!* The next shot is short, giving the Germans the coordinates necessary for the third shell.

Swallowing hard, Smith and his group send a hailstorm of bullets straight for the German officers in the staff car. The car explodes, and metal flies high into the air. A gasoline fire sends flames after the steel. The Canadians shift to their new target and continue the storm on the second tank, which also blows up in a rumble of thunder and torrent of flames. The German soldiers crouch low behind the tanks and fire sporadically; they also toss hand-grenades at the small group.

The two men standing next to Smith are both injured by shrapnel. One is bleeding heavily. Seeing the two men fall, 10 Germans jump out from behind one of the Panthers, rushing the Canadians with guns blazing. Smith is filled with rage. Without hesitation, he runs to meet them head-on in order to protect his fallen comrades.

The enemy's guns are relentless. Grenades explode, and flames light up the area. Smith, yelling at the top of his lungs, bursts through the smoke like a bat out of hell. He plunges at the enemy with the barrel of his gun glowing red-hot. His bullets find soft targets, and in a violent flow of blood, the Germans fall in the rain-drenched mud. Those behind the fallen pause in confusion as Smith screams at them and rushes forward, cutting down anyone in his path. With smoke filling the air around him, Smith fights like 20 men, and what's left of the German foot soldiers retreat to the bushes.

The third tank swivels around and opens fire. Smith continues to fire and scream until finally, the few remaining Germans withdraw down the road. The last tank is bogged down in the mud and abandoned, and is later claimed for use by the Resistance.

Smith runs back to where his friends have fallen and half-carries them to the shelter of a nearby building. Safe for the moment, he binds up the wounds of the pair to stop the bleeding, and then the three wait for the rest of the army, now crossing the bridge in relative safety. Smith earns the nickname "Smokey" for this act of heroism.

Chapter 6
Memories of a Reluctant Hero

P rivate Lloyd Kreamer of Ontario gave up diamond drilling at the Pickle Crow mine to become a sniper-scout with the western regiment of the Princess Patricia's Canadian Light Infantry. Now life has become unexpectedly complicated for Lloyd. He finds himself at the Ausa River crossing during the Battle of the Rimini Line under the direction of the 8th Army. He's in the middle of a shelling tornado that is churning up the river valley and tearing companies apart. Sergeants are taking over from wounded officers, corporals from sergeants, and even privates are called on to take the officers' places. There are no replacements; HQ can't send in new officers. The unit is all they have and everyone's survival depends on his fellow soldiers.

Food is also scarce, with supplies unable to reach the

front lines. Whenever possible, men comb the area for edible plants to put into a communal stew pot.

With the limited resources, reorganization of "B" and "D" Companies into a composite fighting team is necessary, and Lloyd is borrowed from the sniper-scouts to take charge of a section. As the matter is being discussed, a shell explodes squarely in the middle of a trench, killing two, wounding three (including a sergeant), and putting six more out of action. Lloyd, only a metre away from the blast, hits the ground a private and stands back up as the platoon commander, as he is the most senior soldier left in the group.

Realizing that the fate of the wounded is in his hands, and that the men are awaiting orders, Lloyd takes over. After supervising the evacuation of the wounded and reorganizing the men, he reports to the company commander that the platoon is once again "OK and ready to go!"

That night, the Pats cross the San Fortunato Ridge and join the main attack on the Marecchia River so that the Allied army can cross over. It has been raining non-stop all day, and the Germans, now on evacuation alert, have moved most of their heavy artillery over the bridge. With very little resistance from the enemy, the decimated company under Lloyd's command has managed to establish a bridgehead through which the entire New Zealand Division is able to pass.

Next, Lloyd establishes headquarters in a wrecked farmhouse and sets up an all-round defence. His men are hungry and exhausted from the shell and rifle fire, so he organizes a

Private Kreamer (far right) poses for a photo with (from left to right) Cassells, Smythe, and Northwood.

raiding party and liberates an Italian pig from a nearby farm. Soon, Lloyd and his men are feasting on roast pork.

Shortly after the meal, two German vehicles lumber down the road to where the group of Canadians are holed up. The Canadians aren't sure whether to hide or fight. While they are debating the situation, Private George "White Boy" Bowles of Brandon, Manitoba, takes matters into his own hands. Running onto the road in his stocking feet with Lloyd following closely behind, he adopts a silly grin and waves excitedly at the shocked Germans, while yelling greetings in Italian.

The vehicles screech to a stop, and the Germans stare at

this vision in the road, wondering if it's a madman or a ghost. Slamming the cars into reverse, they crash into one another as they try to turn around on the narrow track. Taking to the ditch, the cars bump and bounce back up onto the road and flee in the direction from which they came. Kreamer and White Boy Bowles, rolling with laughter, watch them disappear from sight, then the two Manitobans return to the farmhouse to relay the story to the rest of the men.

Except for a brief interval as platoon sergeant, Lloyd Kreamer remains in command of his group. Finally, after many hardships — including watching the platoon's cook killed by a shell — he has the satisfaction of leading his men over the Marecchia River and on to Celle.

Before the war is over, Lloyd is wounded in the head and leg and is sent home to Canada. Years later, he claims the devil-may-care snipers of the 8th Army were a colourful, swashbuckling crew. Living and fighting by their wits, they considered the battles personal and helped win the war by fighting the enemy one man at a time. When discussing his own part in the war, he says he didn't do anything special. All he did was put one foot in front of the other and hope he didn't step on a mine in the process.

Chapter 7
A Native Canadian Makes the Supreme Sacrifice

B ill "Boots" Bettridge was a sniper with the Queen's Own Rifles of Canada. On Sunday, June 4, 1945, he is aboard the regiment's headquarters ship, the *Hilary*. There is a reverent hush on board. Everyone suspects that they are about to embark on the major invasion that they've all been waiting and preparing for — D-day.

Although everything is ready, the slightest change in weather can throw the entire plan off. The sea is rough, and the wind is whipping down the Solent from the Channel, making everyone nervous. Finally, it's official: due to weather conditions, the incursion is postponed. British, American, and Canadian troops will storm the Normandy coast on

Tuesday, June 6, with most of the Canadians landing on Juno Beach. This is it — the big one.

The *Hilary* lifts anchor at 6 p.m. on June 5. She swings past Cowes and out the Spithead as the bulk of the fleet puts out to sea. The minesweepers are already at work, clearing the mines and marking safe passage for the invasion of the French coast.

The sight of the fleet is a magnificent thing. As England disappears in the sea mist, the ships gather together in an armada that stretches as far as the eye can see. The west wind whistles down the Channel, and even the largest ship in the fleet is rolling in the swells. The sailing lines extend for five kilometres, and each vessel — the largest to the smallest — flies the colours of the Royal Navy.

At 1 a.m. on June 6, the blackened sky masks the silent advance of the darkened ships. The wind howls, swirling noisily around the masts and smokestacks, while below decks the Canadians prepare for battle in eerie blue lights. At 4 a.m., the engines of German aircraft whir in the clouds above. Flares are dropped, lighting up the American portion of the invading fleet. None of the ships responds with gunfire, and the flares eventually burn out. A group of ships this large is impossible to hide, and there is no doubt that the enemy already knows the Allies are coming. Whatever the pilot of the German plane saw in that short burst of light is not worth worrying about.

Again, the sound of engines is heard from the sky.

This time, however, the engines belong to the Royal Air Force's heavy bombers, which are striking at gun positions at Le Havre on the mainland. The bomber stream is so long that while the first planes arrive at the target, others are still taking off from air bases all over England.

As the ships arrive 24 kilometres off the coast, "Action stations!" is called. The airborne troops have already been dropped, and the first wave of infantry regiments prepares to land on the beaches. Hundreds of bombers — Lancasters, Halifaxes, Hurricanes, and their escorts of Spitfires — drop their loads and head back to Britain. For the ships, it's the calm before the storm. The coastline remains silent — threateningly so. The lessons of Dieppe have taught the Allies not to underestimate their enemy. The end has come for the Nazi Regime, but no one expects them to capitulate.

The waiting silence splits open with the first sound of shore batteries firing on the ships. Wireless messages flash throughout the fleet. Leaping forward on the waves, the assault force moves as one, hulls dancing and wakes curling white behind them as they surge forward to the battle with the colours flying. The engines of the planes throb above, and the destroyers' guns fill the fresh ocean breeze with the stench of burnt explosives as the Allies return the enemy fire one for one. This is not a dress rehearsal; this is not Dieppe, Hong Kong, Pearl Harbor, or Dunkirk. Even those who will die on the beaches and the continent as the troops move north can feel victory in the air.

The first hiccup in the invasion comes when the communication of orders is confused and the initial wave of the 3rd Canadian Division troops land on Juno Beach before the tanks. The tanks, waterproofed and fitted with rubber to make them float, are all but useless until they make it onto higher ground. Their job was to land first, dig up the sand to expose the mines, and burst through the barbed wire to make it easier for the infantry to follow. Because the troops have landed first, they are on their own. Mines explode under the crunch of boots, and barbed wire exposes soldiers armed with wire-cutters to the hail of bullets from the enemy.

Boots Bettridge of the Queen's Own lands on Juno Beach with the first wave of assault boats. The door of his landing craft drops, and he hits the cold, chest-high water 90 metres from shore. Each soldier wears about 68 kilograms of gear and sloshes toward the beach with the surf pulling at his legs — that 90 metres seems a good deal farther with bullets whizzing past his head.

Small and large craters on the ocean floor — created by shelling — greet heavy army boots. The men stumble, falling again and again with the forceful surf pounding at them continuously. Struggling to their feet, the Canadians shoot back at the enemy while dodging the bodies of comrades and friends. The lucky make it to the safety of the beach in one piece, and for those veterans of Dieppe, the landing is all too reminiscent of that earlier bloodbath.

Three soldiers carrying a ladder stumble onto the beach

and make a mad dash for the sea wall. The man in the middle steps on a land mine, and no matter how loud the shelling, or the *rat-tat-tat* of gunfire, his death screams jar everyone's senses. And the ladder isn't necessary at all, as the metre-high wall is simply jumped over by the invading troops.

The ensuing maelstrom encompasses all within sight and sound, and time moves quickly, yet stands still. Men seem to be dying in slow motion, and yet the minutes fly by for the soldiers travelling between the boats and the shore. The urgency increases with the intensity of the fighting. The beachhead must be secured or this invasion will fail — and failing would mean the end of the free world.

Boots and four other men — Privates Arsenault, Cooke, Shepherd, and Littlecrow — make it to shore. The battle is personal now, and the excitement of the moment has their hearts pumping in their throats. Adrenalin is flowing. Leaping the wall, the five take cover behind a small sand dune. Every so often, one of them shimmies to the crest of it and dashes forward over the train tracks below, only to be stopped by the rolls of barbed wire and German bullets. Their orders are to move inland, but the men can't comply until the wire is cut. Sergeant-Major Charlie Martin hollers, "Boots, I'm tossing you my wire-cutters. When you get them, throw them to Shep, and tell him to cut a hole through that wire. We'll all go together."

Private Shepherd, hearing his commanding officer, shakes his head and yells, "You go first; you're getting more money than me." There is general snickering, and once the wire-cutters are tossed, they make it safely through the hole.

On the other side, the men are greeted by a minefield. One of them steps on a mine. The man hears the click and stays where he is, motioning for the others to clear out. Once they are far enough away, he jumps clear. The mine doesn't go off right away. Then suddenly it explodes, sending shrapnel in all directions. It hits each of the men, without doing serious harm.

One of the five — Harold Littlecrow — is a Native Canadian. His job as a wireless operator keeps him busy. He passes on valuable information in Cree. The Germans can't decipher the Native language, making it perfect code. The others laugh when they hear him speaking into the mike. They refer to him as Canada's secret weapon.

Because of Harold's important communication role, his companions protect him as much as possible. While they were on board the *Hilary*, Boots had developed a fondness for Harold, finding his compassion appealing and refreshing among the violence and despair they are all experiencing in this war.

The 2nd Canadian Infantry Division lands in Normandy on July 7, after the first wave of troops have moved inland. The front is now approximately 16 to 18 kilometres inland, near Caen. The 2nd Division takes two days to land and reassemble, then works its way through the paths already opened by the previous group.

The 2nd Division sweeps down from the Odon River and attacks the Lebisey woods and chateau at Louvigny, 1.6 kilometres southwest of Caen. Led by Major Jack Anderson of Toronto, the Royal Regiment of Canada joins in the battle. The 3rd Canadian Division flanks their left. The men are travelling through very rough terrain, filled with hills and valleys. From the high ground to their right and left, the men of the 2nd Division are sitting ducks, as mortars pepper the hillside.

Boots's section is ordered into a small group of buildings in No Man's Land (a buffer zone between the two sides). They are told to check for mines and booby traps.

It's approximately 11 a.m. on July 20, 1945. The section finishes loading all necessary equipment, and then Boots drives across a clearing. Seeing the jeep, the enemy begins to shell the area heavily. About halfway through the journey, shrapnel from a mortar explodes through the jeep door and flies right out the other side of the vehicle without injuring anyone.

Upon reaching the village, the group unloads equipment from the jeep and begins hunting for mines and booby traps left by the enemy. The shelling has all but stopped. Leaving the others to do their job in the small village, Boots and his sergeant return to the front.

By 2 p.m., the enemy turns its full attention on the small village and increases the intensity of the barrage. The buildings are being blown to pieces, and Boots climbs into the jeep with his sergeant to go back and pick up his men. Manoeuvring through the narrow, cobblestone streets, he screeches to a stop where he last saw the group. Suddenly, the Canadians, covered in dirt and plaster dust, come running out of a building and jump into the jeep. "Drive! Drive! DRIVE!" they shout, as a group of German soldiers turns the corner with guns blazing.

Seeing an alley in the rear-view mirror, Boots slams the jeep into reverse and floors it, cranking the wheel hard while bullets whiz and ricochet off the jeep. The vehicle twirls in the narrow space, and Boots slams it back into forward while the Germans chase after them. In a flurry of dust and pebbles, the jeep barrels its way to the safety of the surrounding countryside, leaving the chatter of machine-gun fire far behind.

Laughing and joking about their close call, the men check in with their division commander and then drive into an apple orchard to dig in. Harold Littlecrow jumps out of the jeep and begins digging his trench behind the tailgate of the vehicle, while Boots procrastinates. Pulling some fresh socks out of his pack, he sits on the bumper to put them on before starting his own trench. He laughs as he gives Harold a hard time about how deep his trench should be. Suddenly — *whoomph* — an 88 mm artillery shell strikes the rear of the jeep and sends Boots flying through the air to land in Harold's slit trench.

It takes a few moments after the dust settles for the men to realize what has happened. The jeep is demolished with

A Native Canadian Makes the Supreme Sacrifice

Private Shepherd still inside. Privates Arsenault and Cooke lie dead, and Boots discovers he's covered in blood — it is pouring down his hands and legs. He tries to move and almost passes out. He calls out to Harold, then struggles to a half-sitting position. His friend doesn't answer, and Boots feels a chill come over him. Calling out again, he crawls over to where Harold lies. Harold moves and tells him he's okay, just a bit sore in the stomach from the blast.

Harold sees that Boots is bleeding and pulls a field dressing out of his helmet to bind up the worst of Boots's wounds. The pain is intense, and Boots passes out while Harold keeps working to save his life.

Harold yells for medics, struggling to keep his friend alive. He adds pressure to the worst of the wounds to stem the flow of blood and yells again for help. Minutes later, a jeep pulls up, and medics load both men on stretchers. Satisfied that his friend is in good hands, Harold loses consciousness while his hand is still gripping the side of Boots's stretcher.

At the field hospital, neither is expected to make it. Boots has lost too much blood and Harold's stomach wound is too severe for a field hospital to deal with. A padre is called in. Boots, not knowing what's happening, drifts in and out during the last rites.

A few days later, Boots regains consciousness and asks after Harold. He is told that Harold Littlecrow died shortly after receiving last rites.

For the rest of his life, Bill "Boots" Bettridge, will think about his friend. He will always remember Harold's courageous heart and gentle spirit, and the way his love for life and for his fellow men would shine from his eyes when he smiled. Boots will never forget Harold Littlecrow, the man who saved his life.

Chapter 8
The Crawl to Safety

Private Raymond "Tony" Wallace with the 2nd Armoured Brigade is about to take part in one of the greatest armoured and infantry attacks the Canadian Army will make in France. Outside of Falaise, on August 14, 1944, General Crerar tells his troops, "Hit him first and hit him hard and keep on hitting him."

On command, the tanks lumber forward, heading down a hill with orders to close the gap as they approach the outskirts of the town. Tony, inside his tank as it rumbles onward, can feel the excitement building. He's proud to be part of the long awaited D-day — even though the battle has been longer than one day and the fighting for each and every metre of ground has been violent and intense. Tony knows he's on the winning side and that this frontal invasion on the coast of Normandy has finally turned the tide of war against the Germans.

Partway down the hill, there is a loud explosion. The tank ahead of Tony's is hit by an 88 mm anti-tank gun. Tony's tank pulls to a stop and the rest of the platoon visually searches the bushes to see where the shot originated. After a few minutes, Tony's crew is told to get out of there, their tank could be next. However, reluctant to abandon the tank, Tony's decides to take a quick look around.

The next 10 minutes are hard on the nerves as the gun swivels and eyes search the bushes for movement. All of a sudden *whoomph*, and the tank shakes. Dirt and smoke spit everywhere. Stunned for a moment, Tony finds himself on the floor of the tank. He tries to move, but his legs won't do what he wants them to. He realizes he's been hit.

Seconds pass slowly as the dust settles and the smoke clears. All is silent as Tony strains to hear breathing or other normal noises from the rest of the crew. None of his crew makes a noise, and the motor on the tank is silent also. Tony strains to see in the darkness, but can only make out some dark shapes. Then he sees something that turns his blood cold. Close to the turret, an ominous curl of smoke rises upward. Tony can feel the heat inside the vehicle building quickly. In seconds, smoke fills the confines of the tank.

Tony sniffs the air. Mixed with the stench of explosives is the distinct odor of burning electrical wires and fuel. He realizes that the floor of the tank is covered in fuel, as well as his clothes. Within seconds, everything will burst into flames. Pulling himself up on his elbows, he grabs the rungs of the ladder to the top hatch. The smoke is thicker now, and Tony's heart is pounding in his ears. The pain in his legs makes it impossible for him to put any weight on them. By sheer willpower, he uses his arms to pull himself up the ladder and through the escape hatch, dragging his legs behind him. Dropping to the ground, the pain almost makes him pass out. He shakes his head and wills himself to retain consciousness. The tank will soon be engulfed in flames, so he needs to crawl to a safe distance if he has any hope of surviving.

Praying that the snipers haven't seen him, and fighting against the spots dancing before his eyes, Tony begins to drag himself along the ground. After travelling a few paces, he wonders about the rest of his crew. He props himself on his elbows and looks around, but he doesn't see a soul. The other tanks, continuing down the hill, are too far away to see him.

Tony feels sick to his stomach as he realizes he is the only man who made it out of the tank. He tries to pull himself up to his feet, thinking that perhaps if he goes back into the tank he can save one of the others. The pain shoots up his legs and explodes in his head as he collapses onto the ground. He can't even make it to his knees.

By this time, flames are pouring out of the turret hatch. Tony realizes that even if he could get back up there, he'd never find anyone alive with the flames and heat raging inside. He feels helpless, knowing that his comrades — his friends — are still in there and he is unable to do anything but watch.

Tony tears his attention away from the tank. He needs to gain a safer distance before the flames ignite the ammunition inside. Grabbing clumps of grass, he drags himself painfully along the ground. He thinks of his family in Canada, and the image of them receiving the dreaded telegram makes him more determined to survive.

Tony calls out now and again as he pulls himself along, but there's no one to hear him. The Germans are still shelling the area, and with each explosion, pebbles pelt him like a hailstorm. Escaping the tank, he's crawling into the area being mortared by the enemy. Safe from one danger, he's headed straight into another. He looks over his shoulder, trying to identify a safer refuge within crawling distance. But all around him is shelling — there is no safe place. He continues on.

About 140 metres away from the burning tank, he stops and pulls out a field dressing to bind his wounds. He discovers that his left leg is cut in four places and bleeding heavily, but the wounds themselves don't appear too serious. His right leg, however, is serious. Tony can feel that it is broken below the knee, and a huge gash is bleeding freely. Not knowing what else to do, Tony stuffs the hole with a piece of his T-shirt and then uses the field bandages to stem the flow of blood.

With shells and mortars flying overhead, Tony begins crawling once again, praying the whole time that he will be found by someone on the same side as him, and that God will give him the strength to survive. Finally, through the din of battle, he hears voices. Stretching his head up as high as he dares, he sees stretcher-bearers evacuating wounded but has no idea if they are English or German. Realizing that either way he needs medical help, he crawls faster, yelling to get their attention. They don't hear his yelling, and continue loading the wounded onto their jeep, preparing to leave the area. Then, miraculously, the shelling slackens, and a panicked Tony crawls faster and yells louder, waving one hand as high above his head as he can. Finally, an infantryman spots him and runs over to him. As the man calls for the attendants, Tony is relieved to hear him speak English.

The medics make a splint for Tony's right leg out of a rifle. The shelling picks up again, and loading him onto the jeep and strapping the stretcher to the back becomes a risky business. Tony feels vulnerable lying in the open with debris and shrapnel flying from the mortars and shells. But he makes it to the 74th Brigade General Hospital and from there, he is sent back to England. His injuries are serious enough that eventually Tony is sent home to Canada.

The rest of the tanks of the 2nd Armoured Brigade fare better than Tony's. The artillery manages to lay huge smoke-screens to provide cover for the troops, and in the intense heat of the blazing noonday sun, 300 Canadian tanks lead the attack. They sweep down on the Laison Valley to Falaise, churning through it and lunging up the slopes on the far sides. With guns blazing, the tanks, followed by the infantry, punch straight through the German lines and continue up the slopes on the northeast side.

The next day, the Canadians are five kilometres from Falaise and headed toward the rest of Europe. The D-day attack is indeed longer than one day, but it is the beginning of the end of World War II in Europe.

Epilogue
"Lest We Forget"

London, England, is bright and sunny this day in 1943. The hustle and bustle of people on the streets makes the war seem far away — even for Canadian serviceman Gordon Quinn of the Royal Canadian Engineers, who cuts a dashing figure in his army uniform as he waits across the square from Westminster Abbey. Impatient to start his day of hiking in the country with a good friend, he looks at his wristwatch and sees he's early for his rendezvous. He's never been inside the huge stone building, and decides that he has enough time to take a look. So he crosses the square and takes the stone steps of the abbey two at a time.

Through a massive set of doors Gordon enters the gloomy interior of the awe-inspiring building. Above his head, shafts of sunlight pour through the high, leaded glass windows, landing on the stone floor in bright pools. In contrast to the fresh autumn day outside, the building smells dank, musty, old — reminding Gordon of the inside of his town's library back in Canada.

In the foyer, a tour group is gathered, led by an aging clergyman. His thick English accent and slightly worn tweed jacket intrigue the young soldier, and Gordon decides to join the tour. On its way through the ancient halls, the group stops at various tombs of royalty, decorated with statues on stone slabs high on the wall. The tourists look on with interest, some touching the coldness of the carvings and marvelling at the workmanship. On the floor where Gordon walks, he notes with interest the names engraved in the squares below his army boots and smiles as the guide refers to them as "honourable gentlemen."

The group pauses at the famous Poets Corner, and Gordon takes a moment to admire the statue of William Wordsworth. Then, remembering his plans for the day, he looks at his watch and sees his time is up.

Discreetly leaving the tour, Gordon turns and strides down one of the corridors toward the west door exit. Coming to a small cove in the wall, Gordon stops short. A shaft of sunlight is shining on a group of old men in worn clothing, casting an ethereal halo around the silent figures. Standing solemnly with heads bowed and hands behind their backs, they are so still they could have been stone relics. They look as if they're praying as they face the wall of the alcove, and out of respect, Gordon stands quietly, not wanting to disturb their contemplations.

Standing at ease with his military cap in hand, he looks around and notices that the sun is highlighting a stone slab with a row of red poppies carved around the border. The men are facing this stone, and the reverent expressions on their faces touch Gordon. There is a large cross on top of the slab, and at its foot are the words, "He who is known to God alone. Lest we forget."

Finally understanding, Gordon skirts the remembrance stone and quietly moves around the men. He walks out a side door into the brilliant sunshine of the autumn day, and back to the reality of England at war. Across the river, Big Ben strikes 11 — the 11th hour, the 11th day, the 11th month. Gordon pauses to reflect not only on those who died during the Great War, but also on his fellow Canadians who have already died during this one. He prays that no one will ever forget those who died for their countries.

* * *

Louis Therian met me with a huge smile at the door of his Winnipeg home. A man of average height, he went up the stairs before me with an obvious limp, and he huffed and puffed a little after sitting in his recliner. A grandfatherly type, he was still obviously a powerful man.

By the end of our two-hour interview, I had seen a side to him that few people know existed. He showed me the bayonet wound in his upper thigh — after 60 years it is still big enough to put a fist into. He showed me his medals — his German souvenirs. He kept them all wrapped together in a piece of cloth and a small drawstring bag. He said he never took them out, didn't know why he kept them, but couldn't bring himself to throw them away. Most of the mementos, including a couple of St. Christopher medals, he had taken off the bodies of dead enemy soldiers. He looked at me with sadness in his eyes.

"If it wasn't for war," he said, "these men might be alive even today."

I looked at this man with great respect, and I felt a sense of mourning not only for our boys who never made it back, but for all who lost their lives fighting for their respective countries.

Louis wanted to tell me more, but there are some stories, some memories of those days, that can't be shared. For men like Louis, they are as real today as they were 60 years ago, and so is the grief.

Lloyd Kreamer couldn't tell me much of his story. The wound he suffered in the side of his head during World War II had claimed his hearing. Other wounds had made him stiff and sore, and age had done the rest.

His wife had a scrapbook filled with newspaper articles about Lloyd and other Manitobans in the war. She began collecting the articles before she'd even met Lloyd, and had kept them all these years. In the scrapbook are bills from different countries, death notices, and follow-up articles on some of the men after they had returned home.

Some were tragic stories of men who had been gentle and kind, but were subsequently arrested for beating their wives or drinking too much. Some ended their lives in despair, shooting themselves. They are stories of broken men

Epilogue

— medal winners, survivors of horrors that only veterans can truly understand — who found civilian life too hard to bear after seeing the brutal truths of war. Yet so many of these men not only survived war, they survived life after war, raised families, and continue to contribute to our wonderful country.

Fred Snell greeted me in his wheelchair. He spent the first hour of our interview telling me of the heroics of others in his regiment. He showed me his medals and his German pistol. I looked at photos and his books about the Patricias. Most of his story I heard from his wife and read in his papers. It took me almost two hours to pry from him his account of how he saved his platoon from snipers. The only story that hadn't needed prompting was the tale of his daughter when she'd discovered his war service.

None of the men I interviewed enjoyed telling me of their experiences. None was proud of their accomplishments, only amazed at their survival. Some still struggle with the question of why they survived when their buddies, standing next to them, were killed. And for that question, there is no answer. But one thing I discovered through the writing of this book is that in hearing their stories, I will always remember them — and those for whom they mourn.

Further Reading

Jones, Gwilym. *To the Green Fields Beyond: A Soldier's Story.* General Store Publishing House, 1993.

Kee, Robert. *1945: The World We Fought For.* Penguin Books Ltd., 1985.

Mellor, John. *Dieppe: Canada's Forgotten Heroes.* Scarborough, Ontario: Macmillan-NAL Publishing Ltd., 1945.

Munro, Ross. *Gauntlet to Overlord, The Story of the Canadian Army.* The MacMillan Company of Canada Ltd., 1945.

Nicholson, G. W. L. (Lt. Col.) *Official History of the Canadian Army in the Second World War Volume II: "The Canadians in Italy, 1935–1945".* Ottawa: Queen's Printer, 1956.

Parker, R. A. C. *Struggle for Survival The History of the Second World War.* Oxford University Press, 1990.

Reynolds, Quentin. *Raid at Dieppe.* New York: Avon Publications Inc., 1943.

Further Reading

Saunders, Hilary. *Combined Operations — The Official Story of the Commandos.* New York: The MacMillan Company, 1943.

Spencer, Robert A. (Capt.) *History of The Fifteenth Canadian Field Regiment, Royal Canadian Artillery 1941–1945.* Amsterdam: Elsevier, 1945.

Tinkiss Good, Mable. *The Bridge at Dieppe.* Toronto: Griffin House, 1973.

Acknowledgments

I would like to thank all of the veterans who helped me with this book, especially Fred Snell, Lloyd Kreamer, and Norman McCowan of the Manitoba Princess Patricia's Canadian Light Infantry, as well as Louis Therian Sr., who served with Combined Ops in the 8th Army, and Stan Scislowski, who provided me with numerous stories and anecdotes via e-mail. I would also like to acknowledge the veterans I spoke with at the Pro Pats in Victoria, the Transcona, and the St. Vital Winnipeg branches of the Royal Canadian Legion, who prefer to remain anonymous.

My thanks go to Candace Boily who helped with the proofreading and listened to my whining with patience and good humour.

Most of all, I'd like to take this opportunity to thank my editor who helped me with this book, as well as *Unsung Heroes of the Royal Canadian Air Force* and *A War Bride Story*. Thank you Jill Foran; you kept me on track and gave me the much-needed critical eye with diplomacy and never-ending support. I wish you great success in your own writing career.

About the Author

Cynthia Faryon, a mother of three and grandmother of six, began her writing career in 1999 when "Silent Hero" was published in *Homemakers* magazine. Now with five published books to her credit and numerous travel articles, she has future plans to branch out into fiction and full-length biographies.

Besides writing, Cynthia and her husband own and operate a restaurant in rural Manitoba and enjoy being part of small-town Canada.

Photo Credits

Cover: CP PHOTO/National Archives of Canada/Alexander Stirton; page 83: Lloyd Kreamer of Selkirk, Manitoba.

by the same author!

TRUE CANADIAN
AMAZING STORIES™

UNSUNG HEROES OF THE ROYAL CANADIAN AIR FORCE

Incredible Tales of Courage and
Daring During World War II

HISTORY
by Cynthia J. Faryon

ISBN 1-55153-977-2

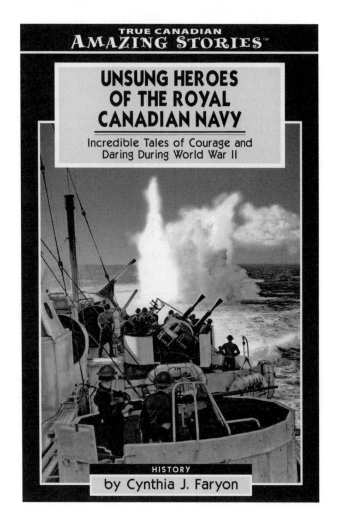

TRUE CANADIAN
AMAZING STORIES™

UNSUNG HEROES
OF THE ROYAL
CANADIAN NAVY

Incredible Tales of Courage and
Daring During World War II

HISTORY
by Cynthia J. Faryon

ISBN 1-55153-765-6

OTHER AMAZING STORIES®

These titles are available wherever you buy books. Visit our web site at **www.amazingstories.ca**

New AMAZING STORIES® titles are published every month.